Praying the Morning Psalms:

Encountering God Through the Six Psalms of Matins

Praying the Morning Psalms:

Encountering God Through the Six Psalms of Matins

A Commentary by an Orthodox Deacon

Saint George Greek Orthodox Cathedral

Greenville, South Carolina

2026

ISBN: 979-8-9987486-2-2

Scripture from *The Orthodox Study Bible*

For permissions contact Father Deacon Charles Joiner at
cjoiner@mac.com.

Saint George Greek Orthodox Cathedral
Greenville, South Carolina

Printed in the U.S.A.

Table of Contents

Historical Development of the Six Psalms

Early Christian Origins (3rd–5th Centuries)

From the earliest days of Christianity, the Psalms were at the heart of the Church's prayer life. Early Christian communities inherited the Jewish tradition of praying Psalms regularly at set hours of the day. The Psalms, considered divinely inspired prayer texts, were integral to the rhythm of daily worship, especially morning and evening prayers.

In the **Egyptian Desert (4th Century)**, the **Desert Fathers** (such as **St. Anthony the Great** and **St. Macarius**) cultivated a practice of reciting Psalms as part of their strict ascetical discipline. By the late fourth century, figures such as **St. Basil the Great (†379)** recommended Psalm recitation as central to monastic prayer.

Jerusalem and Palestinian Monastic Influence (4th–5th Centuries)

The systematic use of Psalms in morning prayers developed significantly through the influence of monastic communities in **Jerusalem and Palestine**, particularly in the monastic centers near Jerusalem (e.g., the monasteries around the Holy Sepulchre). Liturgical practices in Jerusalem emphasized prayer at significant moments of the day, especially dawn (Orthros/Matins) and dusk (Vespers).

During this time, Psalms began to be organized into thematic groups, reflecting spiritual states such as penitence, longing for divine help, thanksgiving, and renewal.

Codification in Byzantine Liturgical Practice (6th–9th Centuries)

By the 6th century, especially through the efforts of **St. Sabbas the Sanctified (†532)** at the monastery he founded near Jerusalem (Mar Saba Monastery), the daily office of Orthros became more structured. St. Sabbas's typikon (liturgical rule) greatly influenced the liturgical practices in Constantinople and across the Byzantine Empire.

It was this monastic tradition, consolidated in **Constantinople**, that ultimately formalized the daily use of the **Hexapsalmos**—the Six Psalms—at the beginning of Orthros. By the 9th century, this practice was firmly established throughout the Orthodox world.

The Thinking Behind the Selection of the Six Psalms

The Six Psalms chosen—**Psalm 3, 37 (38), 62 (63), 87 (88), 102 (103), and 142 (143)**—were carefully selected for their thematic coherence and spiritual significance. Their arrangement follows a clear spiritual progression, from distress and repentance to hope, trust, and renewal in God's mercy.

Why These Six Psalms?

1. Spiritual Awakening and Vigilance:
The first **Psalm (Psalm 3)** expresses immediate cries for deliverance and trust in God amid adversity, setting the tone of awakening spiritually at the dawn of a new day.

2. Repentance and Confession:
Psalm 37 (38) and Psalm 87 (88) are penitential, deeply reflecting the spiritual condition of one who recognizes their sinfulness and dependence upon God's mercy. They guide the

worshiper into a state of humility and contrition, critical for spiritual growth.

3. Longing for God's Presence:
Psalm 62 (63) is a heartfelt prayer of longing and yearning for God, reflecting the inner desire to draw near to His presence at the beginning of each new day.

4. Gratitude and Trust in God's Mercy:
Psalm 102 (103) is a Psalm of praise, thanksgiving, and joyful acknowledgment of God's forgiveness, love, and steadfast mercy. It balances penitence with gratitude.

5. Plea for Divine Guidance:
Finally, **Psalm 142 (143)** is a culmination of this spiritual journey—an earnest cry for God's guidance, illumination, and deliverance from enemies both spiritual and earthly.

Liturgical Meaning and Practice

The Six Psalms are prayed in **complete stillness and reverence**, usually with the faithful standing, and the Church is often darkened. The deep silence underscores their solemnity and spiritual importance. During this time, movement and liturgical activity are intentionally minimized, underscoring the seriousness of these Psalms as a spiritual examination of conscience at the start of the day.

According to Orthodox liturgical tradition, these Psalms also prophetically foreshadow the Last Judgment. It is said traditionally that at Christ's return, these Psalms will be recited, marking the final examination of the soul. Thus, the Six Psalms represent both a daily "mini-judgment" before God and a rehearsal for the ultimate accountability of the soul before the Lord.

Significance and Continued Practice Today

Today, the Hexapsalmos remains central in Orthodox worship as a spiritual compass—reminding believers daily of their **need for repentance, humility, gratitude, and divine guidance**. They anchor the faithful in the foundational spiritual truths that orient the day toward God.

Their historical depth, theological richness, and powerful spiritual insight into the human condition and divine mercy have made them an enduring part of Orthodox Christian prayer for centuries.

Although the Psalms are best prayed without analysis—slowly, attentively, and with a still mind—this book necessarily pauses to reflect on their words. This reflection is not offered as a substitute for prayer, nor as a method to master the Psalms intellectually, but as a quiet aid to those who wish to pray them more deeply. Just as one may step back after prayer to consider what has been received, so this commentary seeks to illuminate patterns, images, and themes that might otherwise pass unnoticed. Such reflection is meant to return the reader again to prayer, not to interrupt it, helping the words of the Psalms descend more readily from the mind into the heart. The hope is that understanding, offered humbly and sparingly, will clear the way for stillness, allowing the Psalms themselves to speak with greater clarity and resonance in the life of daily prayer.

PSALM 3

*1 A psalm by David,
when he fled from the face of his son, Absalom.*

*2 O Lord, why do those who afflict me multiply?
Many are those who rise up against me.*

*3 Many are those who say to my soul,
"There is no salvation for him in his God."*

(Pause)

*4 But You, O Lord, are my protector,
My glory and the One who lifts up my head.*

*5 I cried to the Lord with my voice,
And He heard me from His holy hill.*

(Pause)

*6 I lay down and slept;
I awoke, for the Lord will help me.*

*7 I will not be afraid of ten thousands of people
Who set themselves against me all around.*

*8 Arise, O Lord, and save me, O my God,
For You struck all those who were foolishly at enmity with me;
You broke the teeth of sinners.*

9 Salvation is of the Lord,
And Your blessing is upon Your people.

This Psalm is attributed to King David during his painful flight from his son Absalom (2 Samuel 15–18). As you pray this Psalm, you are praying with the heart of one who is struggling spiritually, seeking a clear relationship with God, inundated with passions and fears—yet clinging firmly to hope in God's help and mercy. This Psalm speaks not just to David's external trials but to your own inner spiritual warfare: the assaults of temptation, fear, and despair.

This Psalm is especially fitting for your morning prayers. The verse about awakening reminds you that every new day is a gift from God—a rising from the night's sleep that echoes Christ's Resurrection. As you begin your day, Psalm 3 teaches you to praise God and place your trust in His protection.

When you pray this Psalm with faith and attentiveness, it becomes more than a historical account—it becomes your own cry, your own confession, and your own act of trust in the Lord who saves.

Commentary

1. A Psalm of David, when he fled from Absalom his son.

2. O Lord, why do those who afflict me multiply? Many are those who rise up against me.

You are called to prayer each morning to align your soul with God's grace. You begin by bringing your attention inward, recognizing that there are many forces that can keep you separated from God. Don't first think of physical enemies around you, but think about your thoughts, temptations, and passions that rise up and war against your soul. This Psalm invites you to reflect on the spiritual struggle that confronts you every day.

Perhaps you've noticed this spiritual war taking place during prayer when your mind starts to drift. Instead of seeking God, you find yourself consumed with worldly concerns, anxieties, and lesser things. These distractions can seem harmless at first, but they steal away the spiritual benefit that prayer offers. They crowd your heart, making it harder to focus, to repent, and to feel God's nearness.

At times, it may even feel like there's a barrier inside your mind, a wall between you and God. That wall can seem impenetrable, especially when you want to pray, when you're trying to repent. And so, like David, you ask: Why? Why do these distractions and temptations multiply the more I try to come close to God? Is it my laziness or my failure to reject them forcefully? Or is it because I'm still trying to fight this battle without fully relying on God's help?

Even asking these questions reveals something important: it shows that your heart is beginning to humble itself, as you begin to cry out sincerely for God's mercy.

In the historical setting of this Psalm, David was overwhelmed by external foes—his own son Absalom had rebelled, turning many against him. David's friends betrayed him. Tribes who once honored him now sought his downfall. He fled from Jerusalem in sorrow and humiliation, uncertain whom to trust.

But the spiritual interpretation, as taught by the Church Fathers, reveals a deeper reality. The foes that multiply and afflict you are:

- The passions—pride, lust, envy, gluttony, anger, sloth, despair—rising within to overwhelm the soul.
- Demons—spiritual enemies who intensify their attacks as you begin to pray, fast, and draw nearer to Christ.
- The world—its empty promises, its distractions, its scorn for faith and holiness.

So when you pray this Psalm, you're not just recalling David's trouble—you're entering into your own. You're standing before God with honesty and saying:

"Lord, the foes within me are many. My heart is restless. My thoughts betray me. My soul feels far from You. But I turn to You now. Deliver me—not just from outer dangers, but from the darkness within. Have mercy. Help me stand. Help me pray. Help me trust You again."

Recognizing how many passions and thoughts rise up against your soul each day, you may begin to wonder: Why do these same struggles keep returning? Why do pride, distraction, envy, fear, or self-indulgence seem to have such power over me? They appear endless, multiplying even as you try to pray or seek God more sincerely.

One reason may be spiritual laziness—the quiet and subtle habit of allowing them to remain, treating them as normal, or even as necessary parts of your personality. If you let this happen, you become complacent and stop recognizing them for what they truly are: foes of your soul. Do not allow yourself—or others—to excuse or tolerate them, or they will gradually gain strength and take deeper root within you. You must seek God's help to confront them.

You may not even realize it, but deep down, you might fear that confronting these passions could shatter your self-image—an illusion of self-sufficiency or personal goodness shaped by a secular worldview. Ask yourself honestly: Am I protecting a false version of who I think I am? Do I really see reality as it is—where the physical and the spiritual are one, where nothing in my inner life is hidden from God? Am I afraid to admit how weak I truly am without His help? These questions are difficult, but if asked sincerely, they become the doorway to repentance and the beginning of true healing.

Like David, you must learn to name these passions for what they are—not harmless habits, not quirks or personality traits, but spiritual adversaries rising up against your soul, your foes. They are not neutral. They war against your peace, your humility, your prayer, and your communion with God. They separate you from God.

Yet this Psalm is not a cry of defeat—it is a plea for divine help. And in praying it, you are already beginning to resist your enemies. You are turning your eyes away from yourself and toward the One who alone can lift you out of confusion, break the power of these passions, and restore clarity, strength, and mercy to your soul.

3. Many are those who say to my soul, "There is no salvation for him in his God."

This verse expresses the challenge of maintaining faith and trust in God's salvation amidst discouraging circumstances found in a secular society where what is considered spiritual is not as true as material things. Worldly affairs dominate and overpower our spiritual concerns. Many don't believe in evil forces, demons, or the devil. Today, we tend to think that it is our will that is the only force at work. In reality, you are continually under attack by evil forces, seeking to discourage you or tempt you into disobedience to what you have been taught.

Paul so clearly expressed the reality of this struggle. He writes,

> "For I do not do the good I want, but the evil I do not want is what I keep on doing… So I find it to be a law that when I want to do right, evil lies close at hand. But I see in my members another law waging war against the law of my mind…" (Romans 19-23)

He recognizes that there is some other force working within him, a force that he cannot fully control or understand, one that keeps him from doing God's will. He knows he has a desire for good, but he sees that his flesh is weak and prone to temptation.

Sometimes, these temptations are subtle, and it can be difficult to recognize them. Acknowledging that your relationship with God could be in jeopardy is unsettling—it exposes your vulnerability and the seriousness of your choices. As you pray this verse, let it awaken your heart. Allow it to stir you to rise above spiritual laziness and self-centeredness, to reject the worldly wisdom that mocks faith, and to align your will fully with the Holy Spirit, cooperating with God's grace.

David experienced the anguish of being mocked by enemies who claimed that even God had abandoned him. For David, salvation was not a vague hope—it was rooted in trust. He believed deeply in the covenantal promises God made to Abraham, Isaac, Jacob, and Moses. Salvation meant placing his hope in God's steadfast love and loyalty. David believed with certainty that God would not abandon His people, no matter how dark the trial. He did not filter his understanding through the skeptical, secular worldview that surrounds you today. For David, the spiritual realm was as real and present as the visible world.

So when you pray this verse, be aware of the sacramental nature of reality and recognize like Paul, there are hidden forces that may lead you to a place where there is no salvation for you.

4. But You, O Lord, are my protector, My glory and the One who lifts up my head.

Seeing God as *"my protector, my glory,"* gives you hope. Addressing God as your shield, you are choosing to seek His protection rather than relying solely on your own will and understanding. When your faith is strong, God's presence naturally guides your actions to overcome evil. But when you struggle to trust Him, it reveals a weakness in faith—one shaped by the worldly mindset of your upbringing, by external or internal voices that cast doubt on God's loving care.

The phrase *"One who lifts up my head"* is especially powerful. It portrays the Lord as the one who restores your courage when you are downcast, your dignity when you feel shamed, and your strength when you are bowed by grief or failure. This image is deeply treasured in the Orthodox tradition, teaching that divine grace—not human effort or reputation—restores your worth and renews your spiritual awareness. When your head is bowed low from sorrow, guilt, or fatigue, it is God who gently lifts it. He calls you to rise—not in pride, but in renewed trust and clarity.

So as you pray this, let God lift up your head. Let Him raise your thoughts beyond the empty lessons of the world and draw you into the truth that can only be found in Him. He is your shield. Trust Him. Follow Him. And allow Him to restore you.

5. I cried to the Lord with my voice, And He heard me from His holy hill.

Making an urgent plea, *"I cried to the Lord with my voice,"* you express your complete dependence on God as a protector. This reflects a turning away from self-reliance that our culture teaches us from a very early age, and instead reaching toward and embracing God's mercy. As you pray these words, you must not merely whisper or repeat these words mechanically—cry out from the depths of your heart, with your voice and your whole being, firmly believing that when you call upon the Lord, He truly hears you.

"His holy hill" refers first to Mount Zion, where the Ark of the Covenant rested, symbolizing God's presence among His people. But in a deeper, mystical sense, it points to Christ Himself and to His Church—the living presence of God on Earth. From this holy mountain, from this place of divine communion, God hears the cries of your heart.

With the words *"He heard me,"* you are embracing God's active presence—His willingness and desire to respond when you pray with sincerity. Orthodox spirituality teaches you to trust in His compassionate attentiveness. A heartfelt prayer is never ignored, even when His response is not immediate or obvious. As you pray, trust that He hears you, and wait patiently upon Him in faith.

6. I lay down and slept;
I awoke, for the Lord will help me.

In this verse, you are not only recalling a night of rest—you are expressing confidence that, upon waking, God will be there to support and protect you. This is why the Church offers this verse in the morning service of Orthros. It teaches you to begin each day with gratitude, knowing that your waking is a gift and a sign of God's sustaining and protective grace.

This verse also carries profound mystical meaning. In the language of the Church, your sleep is a symbol of death, and your rising in the morning prefigures the Resurrection. You are reminded that each day is a miniature Pascha—a rising from darkness into light, from death into life. When you offer your sleep to God in faith, it becomes more than rest—it becomes a quiet act of trust in His protection, His mercy, and His promise to raise you up again.

Think of David. He likely lay down to sleep in caves or beneath cliffs, exposed to the cold night air, guarded only by a few faithful companions. The Judean wilderness east of Jerusalem is a harsh and desolate place—rocky, dry, filled with wild animals and the dangers of exposure. Yet David slept in peace, not because of physical security, but because of his trust in God. When you, too, feel exposed—worn out by life, afraid of what tomorrow holds, or burdened by uncertainty—this is how you must sleep: not in fear, but in full reliance on the Lord.

Throughout Scripture, the wilderness is a place of trial, but also of encounter. This is the environment of the secular society that you experience as this wilderness. It is in your daily activities where God meets the soul in hidden ways, pride is broken, and false supports fall away. Your own wilderness may not be physical—it may be emotional, relational, or even spiritual. But in your everyday life, you are invited into humility, surrender, and deeper trust. Like David, you are called to rest not in comfort, but in the confidence that God watches over you and can guide you.

Your daily "wilderness" foreshadows Christ's own suffering. Jesus also passed through the valley east of Jerusalem—the Kidron—and entered Gethsemane, where He faced betrayal and agony before the Cross. When you sleep in prayer and trust, even when burdened by sorrow, you are joining Christ in His surrender to the Father's will. You, too, may say with Him: "Into Thy hands I commend my spirit," and find peace beneath the shelter of His love.

7. I will not be afraid of ten thousands of people Who set themselves against me all around.

The struggle in your spiritual life often feels like a confrontation with *"ten thousands"* of temptations. Even when you attempt to concentrate on God alone, you may quickly notice how many times your mind fails to remain focused during prayer—how it drifts toward thoughts that have no spiritual value, consumed instead with worldly concerns. These thoughts may not always be sinful in themselves, but they become spiritually harmful when they draw you away from prayer and communion with God. In such moments, your attention is diverted, your prayer falters, and your soul becomes isolated from the grace it seeks. These distractions are not harmless—they are real spiritual enemies.

Historically, David is referring to the overwhelming army of his son Absalom, whose forces vastly outnumbered his own small band of loyal companions. David was not speaking figuratively—he truly faced the threat of death, humiliation, and the collapse of all he had been given. He endured not only physical danger but also the emotional pain of betrayal by his own son and once-trusted advisors like Ahithophel. The loss of the throne would not only be a personal fall but also, in David's eyes, a loss of the divine favor and calling placed on him when he was anointed king.

Yet in the face of this immense pressure and sorrow, David declares, *"I will not be afraid."* His confidence does not arise from human strength or strategy but from total trust in the presence and protection of God. He rests in God's covenant—His enduring love, mercy, and care. David had learned to trust this through many trials: whether in facing Goliath, fleeing Saul, or enduring countless battles, he had experienced God's deliverance again and again. These memories became a source of courage and stability in the storm.

For you as an Orthodox Christian, the *"ten thousands"* symbolize the invisible spiritual warfare waged by temptations, passions, and demonic forces. These surround you, press in on your thoughts, and try to shake your trust in God. But like David, you are called to say with boldness, *"I will not be afraid."* You are not alone. Christ Himself, whom David prefigures, faced betrayal, abandonment, and death without fear, trusting entirely in the Father's will. His victory over the grave is your assurance that no trial is too great when you abide in Him.

Let your confidence be rooted not in your abilities but in God's faithfulness. Stand firm in prayer, and even when surrounded by trials, trust that God is your shield, your glory, and the lifter up of your head.

8. Arise, O Lord, and save me, O my God, For You struck all those who were foolishly at enmity with me; You broke the teeth of sinners.

"Arise, O Lord," is an urgent call for God to intervene—to act now and not delay. This isn't because God is literally inactive or asleep, but rather it is the language of earnest appeal, expressing your deep longing for His immediate help and visible protection. You are asking Him to defend you, to come forth in power and scatter the forces set against you.

This cry echoes the ancient prayer of Moses in the wilderness—*"Arise, O Lord, and let Your enemies be scattered"* (Numbers 10:35)—a prayer repeated by Joshua and the people of Israel as they moved under God's protection. David intentionally uses this same language, linking your present plea to God's mighty acts in history. When you say these words, you are aligning yourself with generations of the faithful who have called upon God in the face of overwhelming odds, trusting Him to act.

The Church Fathers see in this verse a prophetic reference to Christ's Resurrection—God truly "arising" to defeat the ultimate enemies: sin, death, and the devil. So when you pray this verse, you are not only asking for deliverance from present struggles but also participating in the triumphant cry of Pascha: "Christ is risen!"

David speaks of enemies who oppose him *"without cause."* He is not claiming sinlessness, but pointing out that those who rise against him—especially his own son Absalom and trusted companions—do so without justice. He had not provoked them, and their rebellion was rooted in deceit and pride. Spiritually, this reflects Christ Himself, who was betrayed, slandered, and crucified without cause. He bore all this in perfect innocence, offering Himself as a sacrifice for those who hated Him unjustly.

You, too, may face unjust accusations, hostility, or spiritual attacks for your faith. In such moments, this verse becomes your own cry—affirming that God sees your innocence and will be your vindication.

David's image of God breaking the teeth of sinners is vivid and powerful. Teeth in biblical language often represent violence, power, and the ability to devour or destroy—like lions, wolves, or wild beasts. To break their teeth is to strip them of strength and make them powerless to harm you. For you, this image points to God's power to neutralize the destructive influence of sin, temptation, and demonic forces.

In Orthodox spirituality, "teeth" symbolize not only external enemies but the internal passions and spiritual aggressions that gnash at the soul—anger, lust, pride, fear. By God's grace, their power is broken. Through prayer, repentance, and the Cross of Christ, you are no longer at their mercy. They may still snarl, but they cannot devour.

So pray with boldness. You are calling upon the risen Lord, who has already shattered the power of evil. Trust that He hears you. Trust that He defends you. And trust that no matter how many enemies surround you—seen or unseen—they are no match for the One who has truly arisen and broken their strength forever.

9. Salvation is of the Lord,
And Your blessing is upon Your people.

"Salvation (σωτηρία) is of the Lord" affirms with conviction that your salvation comes from the Lord alone. No matter how much you strive, your own effort will never be sufficient without God's grace. Salvation is not something you can earn—it is a divine gift, freely given to those who in humility turn to God in faith, repentance, and love.

Yet this does not mean you can remain passive. You must cooperate with God's grace as you struggle against your sinful tendencies and align your will with His.

This synergy—your willing effort joined to divine help—is at the heart of Orthodox spiritual life. You labor, but you do so knowing that it is the Lord who saves.

David, in his humility, acknowledges that salvation is not the result of his military strength or personal righteousness, but of God's mercy and power. In the same way, you must learn to entrust your life fully to the Lord, confident that His blessing rests upon His people—even in the midst of trials, betrayal, or fear.

This verse is not just a personal affirmation—it is a liturgical and communal truth. Salvation is found in Christ and is poured out through His Church, through the sacraments, and through the life of prayer and repentance. His blessing—His divine favor and presence—is always upon the faithful, sustaining them in every circumstance and leading them toward the Kingdom.

Conclusion

When you pray Psalm 3, you are not merely reciting ancient words—you are stepping into the battlefield of your own soul. You are brought face to face with the inner war: distractions, fears, temptations, and passions that rise against you like an army. But you do not need to face them alone. God is always with you.

This Psalm trains you to cry out—not with passive resignation, but with confidence in God's presence and power. You learn to acknowledge your weakness without despair, to name your enemies without fear, and to surrender your struggle to the One who hears, who rises to save, and who blesses His people.

Through each verse, you journey from confusion to clarity, from fear to trust, from turmoil to peace. You come to understand that salvation is not your achievement, but God's gift. You begin to believe again that He hears you from His holy mountain—that Christ, who once slept in death, now watches over you in resurrection light.

So let this Psalm shape your prayers. Let it draw honesty from your heart and trust from your soul. And let it lead you to that still place where, even surrounded by ten thousand trials, you can lie down and sleep in peace—because the Lord sustains you, lifts your head, and blesses you with His salvation.

PSALM 37 (38)

1 A psalm by David; for remembrance concerning the Sabbath.

2 O Lord, do not rebuke me in Your wrath,
nor chasten me in Your anger.

3 For Your arrows are fixed in me, And Your hand rests on me;

4 There is no healing in my flesh because of Your wrath;
There is no peace in my bones because of my sins.

5 For my transgressions rise up over my head;
Like a heavy burden they are heavy on me.

6 My wounds grow foul and fester Because of my folly.

7 I suffer misery, and I am utterly bowed down;
I go all the day long with a sad face.

8 For my loins are filled with mockeries,
And there is no healing in my flesh.

9 I am afflicted and greatly humbled;
I roar because of the groaning of my heart.

10 O Lord, all my desire is before You,
And my groaning is not hidden from You.

11 My heart is troubled; my strength fails me,
And the light of my eyes, even this is not with me.

12 My friends and neighbors draw near and stand against me,
And my near of kin stand far off;

13 And those who seek my soul use violence,
And those who seek evil for me speak folly;
And they meditate on deceit all the day long.

14 But I like a deaf man do not hear,
And I am like a mute who does not open his mouth.

15 I am like a man who does not hear,
And who has no reproofs in his mouth.

16 For in You, O Lord, I hope; You will hear, O Lord my God.

17 For I said, "Let not my enemies rejoice over me,
For when my foot was shaken, they boasted against me."

18 For I am ready for wounds,
And my pain is continually with me.

19 For I will declare my transgression,
And I will be anxious about my sin.

20 But my enemies live, and are become stronger than I;
And those who hate me unjustly are multiplied;

21 Those who repaid me evil for good
Slandered me, because I pursue righteousness;
And they threw away my love as though it were a stinking corpse.

22 Do not forsake me, O Lord;
O my God, do not depart from me;

23 Give heed to help me, O Lord of my salvation.

Psalm 37 (38) is a cry of repentance—a raw, unfiltered outpouring of sorrow, shame, and longing for healing. As you reflect on this psalm, you're not just reading David's confession; you are invited to step into his shoes and feel the weight of your own sin pressing on your heart, your body, and your soul. This is not abstract theology—it's a wounded prayer that you, too, can pray when you feel broken, when guilt overwhelms you, and when your heart aches for God's mercy. Through this Psalm, you are called to face the pain of being separated from God, to see clearly the damage that the nature of your sinfulness has done, and to weep with holy sorrow. But don't stop there. This is not a descent into despair—it's the first step toward transformation. As you turn back to God, with honesty and humility, you begin to rediscover the healing that comes through repentance. This Psalm reveals the great love Christ has for mankind. It shows you your way back to the One who alone can restore your soul to a union with God.

Commentary:

1. A Psalm by David; for remembrance concerning the Sabbath

**2. O Lord, do not rebuke me in Your wrath,
nor chasten me in Your anger.**

This Psalm begins with your cry for mercy—but before you can truly seek it, you must become deeply aware of your own sinfulness. That's how it was for David.

He was spiritually asleep until the Prophet Nathan awakened him to the gravity of his actions (2 Kings 12 LXX–2 Samuel 12). Nathan didn't begin with accusation. He told a parable—a wise and compassionate way to pierce through David's defenses:

Nathan's Parable:

> "There were two men in a city: one rich, and the other poor. The rich man had many flocks and herds, but the poor man had nothing but one little ewe lamb, which he loved dearly. A traveler came to the rich man, and instead of taking from his own flock, he took the poor man's lamb and prepared it for his guest."

You can almost feel David's righteous fury as he hears this. He declares the rich man deserves death. And then Nathan speaks the words that cut straight to the heart: "You are the man."

So now, as you read this Psalm, put yourself in David's place. You, too, are asked to look honestly at your heart. Often, your faults and passions hide beneath layers of pride. You may not see them clearly. But that hiddenness doesn't make them harmless. It makes them more dangerous. Your pride wants to preserve the illusion of righteousness. It resists confession, avoids exposure, and clings to self-justification. Yet unless you let God uncover your condition, you cannot be healed, perfected, or made worthy of eternal life with Him.

True repentance begins when you humble your heart—when you let the light of God's truth search the dark and neglected places of your soul. Only then can you see your sin clearly. Only then can you begin to seek not just forgiveness, but correction and restoration—the mercy that prepares you for eternal life.

You may wrestle with the idea of God's anger. Isn't God love? Yes—always. But Scripture often uses human language—what the Fathers call anthropomorphisms—to help you grasp divine realities. When Scripture speaks of God's "anger," it doesn't mean

God changes or loses control. It expresses the pain and disruption that you feel when you separate yourself from Him. Sin creates distance. That distance, that inner ache, that turmoil—that is what we experience as divine "wrath."

St. John Chrysostom helps you understand: God's "wrath" is not like human wrath, which is passionate and reactive. God's correction is never without purpose. He allows you to taste the consequences of your actions so that you might be brought to repentance. In Chrysostom's words:

> "He chastises not out of hatred but to amend—not merely to punish but to correct. The wrath of God revealed from heaven is not directed against individuals but against all ungodliness and unrighteousness; it seeks not destruction but correction and salvation." (See Chrysostom's Homily III on Romans 1:18)

So when you feel the weight of your guilt, don't despair. Do what David did— plead for mercy. Ask that God not rebuke you in His wrath, but discipline you gently, with compassion. Know that even when you feel the pain of God's correction, it is not rejection. It is love—pure, holy, perfect love—drawing you back into communion with Him.

Like David, you must learn to trust in God's compassionate and forgiving nature. Don't hide. Don't excuse. Come forward and say, "Have mercy on me, O Lord. Do not rebuke me in Your wrath."

And may that be your daily prayer—for all your failings, for all your thoughts and actions, known and unknown. Seek His mercy, and trust that He will not turn away from a heart that is humble and broken before Him.

3. For Your arrows are fixed in me, And Your hand rests on me;

"For Your arrows are fixed in me": When you truly recognize your sins, it can feel like a piercing pain in the heart—a sudden and painful realization: "I have done wrong before God." Like an arrow wounding the flesh, it is not a surface-level regret, but a deep inner wounding—not from condemnation, but from the soul's awakening to the truth.

This recognition of sin does not leave the soul in despair. Instead, it creates a yearning for healing, a longing to return to communion with God. Just as David vividly expresses how deeply the awareness of his sin wounded his conscience, so you must also awaken to your own sinfulness and feel the pangs of sorrow— the arrows that God mercifully sends into your heart to pierce you with moral conviction.

"Your hand rests heavily on me": Sin has the power to separate you from God's grace and His heavenly kingdom. David's condition felt like a heavy burden pressing upon him, and your own conscience should feel that same heaviness, grief, and sorrow. This echoes the words of Christ in the Beatitudes:

> "Blessed are they that mourn, for they shall be comforted." (Matt. 5:4)

Such mourning is not despair, but a loving, corrective discipline—not punishment, but an urgent call to repentance and transformation.

Pay close attention to this spiritual heaviness and allow it to move you toward change. You will need humility, and must willingly acknowledge that the burden of sin is too heavy to carry alone. You must rely completely on God's help.

In this way, God's loving correction leads you not to shame, but to repentance, and through repentance, to restoration—a restoration that comes through confession, healing, and renewed communion with Him.

**4. There is no healing in my flesh because
of Your wrath;
There is no peace in my bones because of my sins.
There is no soundness (ὑγίεια) in my flesh because
of Thy indignation (ὀργή); there is no health (ἴασις)
in my bones because of my sin.**

Your sinfulness is like an illness that affects not only your spirit but also your body. Spiritual wounds can manifest as physical suffering—restlessness, anxiety, fatigue—and they can only be healed through God's mercy and grace. In today's world, you may often seek medical or psychological treatment rather than recognizing the spiritual cause.

The mention of *"bones"* in the Psalms signifies that sin penetrates to the deepest core of your being. When inner health or peace (ἴασις) is lost, you become vulnerable to spiritual unrest, anxiety, and distress, all of which disturb the very foundation of your life. When sin breaks your communion with God, it causes a kind of internal anguish, leaving you shaken, unsettled, and profoundly troubled at the core.

But there is healing (ὑγίεια) in turning back to God in humility and repentance to find true health and restoration. Repentance is the cure—not merely a sorrowful feeling, but a return to the source of life.

As Elder Aimilianos writes:

> "When a person repents, he becomes conscious of God's love. He does not despair; he does not become downcast or depressed. He knows how to stand before God and say: 'God, I'm wrong. Tell me what to do—not so that I might pay for my crime'—God does not demand such 'lament' from us—'but so that I might be corrected and healed.'"

This is the true purpose of repentance: not punishment, but healing. To stand before God honestly, seeking not judgment, but renewal, is the path to wholeness of both soul and body.

5. For my transgressions rise up over my head; Like a heavy burden, they are heavy on me.

"For my transgressions rise up over my head": This verse describes sin as overwhelming, heavy, and impossible to bear without God's mercy and help—like floodwaters rising above your head, suggesting drowning, suffocation, and spiritual helplessness. This is the kind of inner weight experienced when you become truly aware of your sinfulness and its consequences. It is not merely a sense of guilt over a single act, but a deep realization of how numerous and serious your sins are, and how powerless you are to overcome them without divine grace. The closer you come to God, the greater is the reality of your sinful nature in the eyes of Christ.

You must also understand that sin is not just a mistake or personal flaw. From God's perspective, it is a spiritual crime—a rupture in a relationship grounded in love. In sinning, you place yourself above God's will and reject His divine order. You grasp at glory that does not belong to the sinner, but to the one who, through humility and repentance, is transformed and restored in communion with God.

6. My wounds grow foul and fester because of my folly.

David sees himself clearly, describing spiritual wounds that worsen without repentance.

Your sins are like bruises or open sores on your soul. Just as untreated bodily wounds can become infected and begin to fester, sin, if ignored, will spread and corrupt your entire soul. Thus, your sins urgently require healing before corruption overtakes you.

Sin, when left unaddressed by repentance, confession, and spiritual healing, gradually corrodes your soul, creating deeper spiritual harm and disorder. The Physician of your soul is Jesus Christ, who brings healing through sincere repentance and heartfelt confession, based on genuine humility. Only by humbly acknowledging your desperate need for His mercy and healing can your soul be fully restored.

7. I suffer misery, and I am utterly bowed down; I go all the day long with a sad face.

"*I am utterly bowed down (ἐταπεινώθην):*" David is expressing that his humility and sorrow for sin have brought him low. He is deeply mourning the consequences of his sinfulness. This is how you too will feel when your sinful nature is acknowledged and your soul bears the weight of your condition.

"*I go all the day long with a sad face (σκυθρωπάζων)*" means to be profoundly unhappy, miserable, and afflicted by inner torment. It's an outward expression of grief. Like David, you must recognize your own brokenness—acknowledge the emptiness that causes a separation of you from communion with God.

Like David, you should sincerely and humbly recognize that this sorrow comes from your own actions, which have disappointed the God you love. Because you love Him, this realization should stir within you heartfelt sorrow, moving your conscience to genuine remorse and repentance.

8. For my loins are filled with mockeries, And there is no healing in my flesh.

"Filled with mockeries" indicates intense suffering or anguish like an intense fire—the continual accusing voice of a troubled conscience. This is how you may experience your awareness of your sinfulness before you repent.

The *"loins (γαστήρ)"* in biblical language often refer to a person's strength, vitality, or inner core. The Greek γαστήρ refers to the belly or stomach. So, to be "filled with burning" could symbolize not only emotional or spiritual distress, but also physical suffering and weakness, like an upset stomach that gives an intense discomfort.

"There is no healing (ἰατρεῖον) in my flesh." This expresses an unresolved distress that you feel when you encounter your sinful condition.

Your sin robs you of dignity, strength, and peace, leaving behind shame and humiliation. It activates your conscience to work against you, generating feelings of shame. This is not meant to be suppressed. It can become a path to healing—because through repentance, you are not crushed by your sins, but liberated and restored by the mercy of God.

9. I am afflicted and greatly humbled;
I roar because of the groaning of my heart.

Like David, you may reach a point when the anguish within you can no longer be contained. You feel spiritually wounded, weighed down by guilt, shame, and the pain of being separated from God. The sorrow you carry isn't superficial—it reaches deep into your heart, pressing on the very core of your being. Your inner discomfort becomes a kind of roar, not just a sound of suffering, but a cry rising from the depths of your soul, longing for mercy, forgiveness, and healing.

The "*groaning (στεναγμός) of my heart*" is not poetic language—it's real. It is an inner lament you feel when you look honestly at your condition in relation to God. You may have already acknowledged it, but have not yet brought it fully to God. And the longer you delay, the more that inner unrest grows. This cry is born from resisting God's help, from postponing the moment when you let Him restore your inner peace.

But this cry is also a turning point. When you let it rise, when you pour out your grief to God, it is not a cry of despair—it's a cry of hope. It means you are ready to change. You are ready to come home.

May you, too, cry out to God with this kind of anguish. Trust that He hears you. Trust that He will not turn away. Let this sorrow lead you to the next step: to reach out for the grace of the sacrament of Confession. Seek out a priest for guidance and the sacrament of Confession, not to be judged, but to be healed. This is how the cry of your heart becomes the first step toward peace, restoration, and new life in Christ.

10. O Lord, all my desire is before You, And my groaning is not hidden from You.

With your sin clearly before you and your conscience crying out, you become aware that nothing is hidden from God. You now assume that He knows all your errors and sinful desires. You must not hide anything, so He will not see you as a hypocrite, like Jesus saw the Pharisees.

Like David, you can acknowledge this feeling of nakedness in front of God. It is also a recognition of God's omniscience. You will experience God peering directly into your soul, understanding even your unspoken feelings and hidden pain.

You can find comfort in the truth that God already knows everything about you, including the sincerity of your desires for repentance and the depth of your suffering. Trust in God's compassion, affirming that He understands and cares deeply for the human heart.

11. My heart is troubled; my strength fails me, And the light of my eyes, even this is not with me.

12. My friends and neighbors draw near and stand against me, And my near of kin stand far off;

Until you are ready to confront your condition and seek God's help, your physical and spiritual strength are limited. You may have difficulty sleeping. You, like David, can feel abandoned, drained, and without hope. You will begin to realize that you need to accept God's love and mercy. Sin and suffering isolate David and will also isolate you. Even your friends and family may distance themselves from you in your suffering. David's experience suggests that others are probably also aware of your sinfulness and may even distance themselves from you. But remember that God is always there with his love. This He never withdraws.

Your sins always have consequences. You must muster the strength to act. It is only through repentance that you can be healed through the work of the Holy Spirit by seeking divine help with humility.

13. And those who seek my soul use violence,
    And those who seek evil for me speak folly;
    And they meditate on deceit all the day long.

There seem to be forces at work that continually tempt us, causing us to fall away from our obedience to God's will. You should not be surprised if you experience dire consequences. David committed the most serious sins: adultery with Bathsheba and then orchestrated the death of her husband, Uriah, by placing him at the front of battle. His sin was exposed by the prophet Nathan, who pronounced judgment: *"Now therefore the sword shall never depart from your house..."* (2 Samuel 12:10)

As a result, David suffered many violent consequences: the death of the child born from his sin (2 Samuel 12:14–18); Absalom's rebellion—his own son rose against him violently, humiliating him and threatening his life (2 Samuel 15); Amnon's rape of Tamar, followed by Absalom's murder of Amnon—violence erupted within his own household (2 Samuel 13). These were the natural consequences of the spiritual and moral disorder his sin had unleashed in his family and kingdom.

Your sins have consequences. These are allowed due to the great mercy God has for us. He is always ready to receive us like He received the Prodigal Son (Luke 15:11–32) in his return, if you are able to do so with humility, seeking His forgiveness.

**14. But, I like a deaf man, do not hear,
     And I am like a mute who does not open his mouth.**

**15. I am like a man who does not hear,
     And who has no reproofs in his mouth.**

Become like David, who, as he struggled with the trials of his life, recognizing his errors and their consequences, did not argue, retaliate, or try to justify himself.

Instead, he accepted the reproach in silence, knowing he was guilty and trusting in God for justice and mercy. This Psalm shows you a way to pray for God's mercy with humility. Learn to show this by not reacting out of pride or defensiveness, understanding that it is not your place to defend yourself when you have sinned. Entrust your case to God, the only true Judge. Repent.

The story of Shimei is a powerful real-life example from David's life that beautifully illustrates the humility and silent endurance you must cultivate. Shimei was a relative of King Saul, from the tribe of Benjamin. When David was fleeing Jerusalem during Absalom's rebellion—a time of deep humiliation and suffering— Shimei came out and cursed David openly, throwing stones at him and accusing him of being a murderer and usurper (2 Samuel 16:5–13). One of David's soldiers, Abishai, wanted to kill Shimei for insulting the king, but David stopped him and said: "Let him curse, because the Lord hath said unto him, Curse David... It may be that the Lord will look on my affliction, and that the Lord will requite me good for his cursing this day." (2 Samuel 16:10–12)

Be like David, who refused to defend himself even though all the accusations weren't entirely true. Accept them in silence and humility, recognizing your own sin and the justice of God's discipline when confronted with them. Trust that God in His love and mercy, not man, will be your vindication.

You can also see a parallel of David's actions in the Passion of Christ. When Jesus stood before His accusers (Caiaphas, Pilate, Herod), He remained mostly silent. "He was oppressed, and He was afflicted, yet He opened not His mouth; He was led as a lamb to the slaughter." (Isaiah 53:7) Christ's silence in suffering fulfilled David's words perfectly, showing innocence, meekness, and complete trust in the Father's will.

When you are being slandered or judged for any reason, whether fairly or unfairly, remain silent, realizing that only God is the true judge. This silence is a sign of humility, repentance, and trust in God.

16. For in You, O Lord, I hope;
You will hear, O Lord my God.

"For in You, O Lord, I hope": As you pray this Psalm, express, like David, your trust in God alone, your faith that God will hear your prayers, and provide deliverance. Have patience, because God responds on His own time.

In times of difficulty, you must respond with true faith, maintaining confidence—even in silence—that God will act righteously on your behalf. When you are attacked or mistreated, your response becomes a mirror of your inner spiritual life. You must be patient and take time to examine your faith and ask yourself: "How do I respond in adversity? Do I remain rooted in trust and love, or does this trial reveal a need to strengthen my faith?"

God invites you, even in the midst of trials, to grow in faith—not by taking justice into your own hands, but by entrusting yourself to His perfect will and love, just as David did.

17. For I said, "Let not my enemies rejoice over me, For when my foot was shaken, they boasted against me."

As you strive to live a Christ-like life and begin to recognize your sinful actions, there are many forces in today's society that will try to discourage you, even to defeat or define you. Their subtle accusations or mockery can keep you trapped in shame and prevent your healing—holding you back from progressing spiritually. Instead, you must call on inner strength with God's love in your heart and seek help from God.

David, though vulnerable and repentant, did not allow his enemies to triumph over him. His response, however, was not retaliation—but humility and repentance. He turned to God as his defender.

In the same way, you must respond with repentance, not pride or vengeance. You must ask God to grant you victory over your sinfulness, rather than trying to fight your battles alone. God is the true Judge, and you must entrust judgment to Him.

If you retaliate in pride or anger, you only make enemies and continue the cycle of sin. But if you return to God with a humble heart, with His love He will raise you up and show you the way to respond. Your greatest battle is not against those who accuse you—but against the prideful nature that seeks to enslave you. Only God can give you the victory.

18. For I am ready for wounds,
And my pain is continually with me.

"I am ready for wounds (scourages-μάστιγας)" using the Greek word μάστιγας means whippings or chastisements, often with penitential and disciplinary overtones. It points to the seriousness of the afflictions that can follow sin— whether they take the form of inward spiritual anguish or outward suffering.

These are not meaningless pains, but consequences meant to awaken you to your spiritual condition.

This suggests a readiness to accept God's correction—not in despair, but in humility. The psalmist is not resigning himself to destruction, but offering himself willingly to divine discipline, with sorrow as a constant companion. This posture is profoundly fitting for a penitential Psalm.

Like David, you are called to accept God's correction—not as harsh punishment, but as something just and even necessary. To truly repent is not merely to ask that suffering be taken away, but to ask that it may purify you. In this way, you become spiritually prepared to endure whatever the Lord allows, trusting that His discipline is ultimately for your healing.

In the Orthodox tradition, divine correction is understood not as retribution, but as therapy for the soul. The sorrow you feel is not a sign that God has abandoned you, but that He is drawing near with mercy to restore you. And this sorrow, if embraced in humility and love, is not self-hatred—it is holy compunction. It springs from your love for God, and your grief over having wounded that love.

Such sorrow, when received with trust, becomes the fertile ground of repentance. It softens your heart. It clears your vision. It turns you toward the Father. And in that sorrow, you begin your return—not in despair, but in hope, knowing that even your chastisement is a sign of His mercy.

19. For I will declare my transgression, And I will be anxious about my sin.

This is a crucial moment in your repentance—the moment of confession, when you stop hiding and bring your sin into the light before God. Like David, it is important to come to the point where you can say without hesitation, *"I confess my transgression, I'm sorry."* Don't try to shift the blame or excuse yourself by pointing to your upbringing, your circumstances, or other people. You say *"my transgression"*— owning it completely. This act of personal responsibility is essential for true repentance.

"I will be anxious about my sin" means you are ready to act. You are prepared to do whatever God asks of you to be cleansed, healed, and set free. You're not just looking for relief from guilt—you're seeking restoration. You are saying to God, "Teach me how to change. Lead me into Your ways."

Declaring your sin is not merely about feeling bad. It is a bold, honest step toward healing and renewed communion with God. In the Orthodox Church, this takes form in the sacrament of Confession—not as a ritual of shame, but as a sacred encounter with divine mercy. You speak your sins aloud before God, with a priest as witness and guide, not to be condemned, but to be forgiven and restored.

This is how you must approach confession: with humility and honesty, without excuses, with a heart that is broken yet hopeful.

Be willing to face yourself with God. Be ready not just to be forgiven, but to be transformed. Confession is not the end—it's the beginning of your return to the Father's embrace.

20. But mine enemies live and are become stronger than I; And those who hate me unjustly are multiplied.

Your enemies may take many forms. They could be people who betray you, like Absalom betrayed David. They might be spiritual enemies—temptations or demonic forces—that press harder when you are at your weakest. Or perhaps it's the sting of injustice itself, when those who defy God seem to flourish, at least for a time.

This moment captures the sorrow of being attacked while already bowed low. You're not only burdened by your own guilt—you're also pierced by the pain of being misunderstood, slandered, or rejected. You experience the same tension that so many saints have known: you are truly repenting before God, yet others continue to judge, accuse, or harm you.

Here is a vital truth you must learn: even when you genuinely repent, others may not forgive. Even if you're innocent of what they accuse, they may still hate you. Your comfort cannot rest in being vindicated by others, but in the righteousness and mercy of God, who sees the truth of your heart.

This verse, like many in the Psalms, also points you to Christ. He, too, was hated without cause. His enemies grew in influence. Though perfectly innocent, He bore shame, violence, and betrayal in silence, entrusting all judgment to His Father.

As Christ said, *"They hated Me without a cause."* (John 15:25, quoting Psalm 34:19 LXX)

So in your own moments of sorrow, weakness, and injustice, remain faithful. Let this verse remind you that God sees all things, and your final vindication rests not in the hands of men, but in His. Trust Him to be your defender, and continue on the path of humility, knowing that in His time, all will be made right.

21. Those who repaid me evil for good
Slandered me, because I pursue righteousness;
And they threw away my love as though it were
a stinking corpse.

Like David, you strive to live with righteousness before God—showing kindness, integrity, and justice toward others. Yet despite your efforts, you may still be met with harm, betrayal, slander, or rejection. This kind of injustice wounds deeply.

It's one thing to suffer when you've done wrong—but to be punished for doing good feels especially cruel.

And yet, you're not alone. The saints walked this very path. They were misunderstood, falsely accused, and persecuted—not because they did evil, but because they lived holy lives. St. Paul reminds you of this in Romans 12:21: *"Be not overcome by evil, but overcome evil with good."*

When you suffer for doing what is right, you are sharing in the Cross. It may feel unfair, but it's also a mystery of grace—one that purifies your soul and draws you closer to Christ, who Himself suffered unjustly.

You must also remember: you cannot control how others treat you, nor should you expect them to change. Your goal is not to gain the approval of people, but to be faithful before God. If you act with integrity and love, even when others wrong you, then you are blessed—for you are walking the same path your Lord walked.

In those moments, do not grow bitter. Do not retreat into resentment. Keep your eyes fixed on Christ, and trust that He sees your heart. He knows the truth, and He will not forget your faithfulness.

22. Do not forsake me, O Lord;
O my God, do not depart from me;

23. Give heed to help me, O Lord of my salvation.

Call urgently upon God's faithfulness, placing your complete dependence on His continual presence and mercy. As you reach the end of this Psalm, your heart cries out—not to be forsaken by the Lord—because you know, with certainty, that He alone is the source of your salvation and deliverance.

You no longer want to trust in your own strength or righteousness. You know you cannot save yourself. So you call on the Lord as your only refuge, your only hope. When you say, *"Be attentive,"* it's not a casual request—it's the desperate plea of a soul in distress. You are like a patient reaching for the only true physician, or a drowning person crying out for the one hand that can lift you from the depths.

These final verses show you where true repentance leads—not to despair, not to pride or self-reliance, but to a complete and humble turning toward a loving God. You place your hope in His mercy, not your merit. You look not inward, but upward. And you trust that He is near—that He hears, that He sees, and that He will save.

Let this be your own conclusion when you repent: not sorrow without hope, but sorrow that leads you home.

Summary

This Psalm becomes your own spiritual mirror—a reflection of your journey of repentance, your endurance through trials, your trust in God, and your hope in His mercy and restoration. It invites you to walk the path of healing by first exposing your sin and feeling the weight of your disobedience. That painful awareness is not the end—it is the beginning. It's the first step toward the healing of your soul.

The path to salvation begins when you open your heart to God with a living faith, one rooted not in fear but in love for your Creator. Healing begins when you honestly recognize the sickness within— when you admit your need and freely turn to God as your physician, your cure, and your only hope.

As your sin becomes clear, you begin to feel that deep, piercing sorrow—the kind that tells you something is terribly wrong, that you've wandered from the One who gives life. This is the pain of the heart that urges you to seek reconciliation. And in that pain, the desire for repentance is born.

Your life will not always be steady. There will be times when you walk in the joy of God's presence, and other times when He seems far away. But in truth, He never forgets you—it is you who drift away. Your greatest enemy in this journey is your ego, the false king that rises up and tries to dethrone God from the center of your heart. It resists His will, replaces His love with pride, and leads you into exile.

To return, you must confront this reality within yourself. You must acknowledge your pride, your disobedience, your indifference—all the things that have separated you from Him. This is the path to healing. This is the gift of repentance.

As Archimandrite Aimilianos of Simonopetra says:

> "When I reject the way of repentance, I reject God. When I choose to remain in sin, I expel God from my heart. But as soon as I turn from my sin, God enters my heart. And when He does, I discover my place in the Church, which is His body and His bride."

So read this Psalm not only as your own prayer, but as God's loving cry to you—a divine call to return to Him. He invites you to receive His love, to run back to Him with all your heart. Through repentance, you rediscover your life, your healing, your salvation.

PSALM (63)

A canticle of desire for God—
A message about communion with God

1 A psalm by David, when he was in the desert of Judea. *

2 O God, my God, I rise early to be with You;
My soul thirsts for You.
How often my flesh thirsts for You
In a desolate, impassable, and waterless land.

3 So in the holy place I appear before You,
To see Your power and Your glory.

4 Because Your mercy is better than life, My lips shall praise You.

5 Thus I will bless You in my life;
I will lift up my hands in Your name.

6 May my soul be filled, as if with marrow and fatness,
And my mouth shall sing praise to You with lips filled
with rejoicing.

7 If I remembered You on my bed,
I meditated on You at daybreak;

8 For You are my helper,
And in the shelter of Your wings I will greatly rejoice.

9 My soul follows close behind You;
Your right hand takes hold of me.

10 But they seek for my soul in vain;
They shall go into the lowest parts of the earth.

11 They shall be given over to the edge of the sword;
They shall be a portion for foxes.

12 But the king shall be glad in God;
All who swear by Him shall be praised,
For the mouth that speaks unrighteous things is stopped.

Commentary

When you rise before the sun, before the world has stirred, before your thoughts have gathered and your heart has settled—what do you seek? This Psalm places you in that silent hour, in the wilderness of the soul, where all distractions fall away and one truth remains: you thirst for God.

Psalm 62 (63) is not just a Psalm you read; it's a cry you offer. It teaches you how to pray not with polished words, but with longing—with a heart laid bare, dry, and aching for communion with your Creator. In David's voice, you find your own voice: the voice of a soul exiled from comfort, from certainty, even from the visible presence of God, yet still reaching, still hoping, still clinging.

As you journey through this Psalm, you walk with David into the spiritual wilderness—a place stripped of distractions, where thirst is no longer avoidable and your deepest hunger is uncovered. And in that very place, something remarkable happens: prayer is born. Real prayer. The kind that arises not from obligation, but from desire.

This Psalm is your guide through that journey. It begins with thirst and ends in joy. It teaches you to seek God before anything else, to remember Him on your bed, to bless Him in your daily life, and to trust in His mercy even when surrounded by enemies or afflicted by inner battles. It invites you to cleave to Him—to adhere so closely that nothing can separate you.

Psalm 62 is not simply about words; it is about becoming. As you pray its verses, your soul is reoriented. You learn to see the dawn as a sacred hour. You begin to recognize your soul's thirst as a sign of life. You come to know that God's mercy is better than anything this world calls "life." And, slowly, your soul begins to bless, to lift, to rejoice, and to cling.

Let this commentary be a companion in your early prayers, in your wilderness places, and in those quiet moments when you realize that what you truly seek is not something—but Someone. Let this Psalm awaken in you the truth that communion with God is your purpose, your healing, your joy, and your home.

1. A Psalm by David, when he was in the desert of Judea.

**2. O God, my God, I rise early to be with You;
My soul thirsts for You.
How often my flesh thirsts for You
In a desolate, impassable, and waterless land.**

"O God, my God" You begin with an intimate cry, not a distant or formal address, but a plea born of love, urgency, and deep dependence. Repeating His name isn't just for emphasis—it reveals the closeness you feel, the longing that stirs within you like a child calling out twice in the dark to its mother. You are not merely seeking help or protection—you are seeking communion. Your soul instinctively turns to the One who created it, because you were made for Him.

As St. Augustine once said:

"You have made us for Yourself, O Lord, and our heart is restless until it rests in You." (Confessions, Book 1, Chapter 1)

When you say, "*I rise early to be with You,*" you're describing more than the time of day. You're speaking of a posture of the heart. The Orthros, the final watch of the night before sunrise, has always been a sacred hour in the life of the Church—a time of stillness, clarity, and spiritual watchfulness. This is the moment you seek God: before the noise, before the meals, before even the light. In this quiet hour, your soul is most awake to His presence.

"*My soul thirsts for You*" is not poetic exaggeration. You feel it—it's a yearning deeper than bodily thirst, deeper than any desire for comfort or success. It is the longing for God Himself—not for His gifts, but for His very being. Nothing else—no achievement, no relationship, no pleasure—can satisfy what your soul was made to receive: communion with Him.

And when you pray, "*in a desolate, impassable, and waterless land,*" you speak from the desert (wilderness) of your own heart. Yes, David was in the wilderness of Judah, fleeing from Absalom. But that physical place also reveals something within you. The wilderness mirrors your inner condition when you are far from God—dry, lifeless, desolate. It is the land of the soul when grace feels distant and prayer feels hard. And yet, it is in that very wilderness that something begins to stir.

In the Orthodox tradition, this barren land reflects the fallen world itself— fruitless, thirsty, and empty apart from God. But it is also the place where your soul begins to awaken. You start to feel the thirst. And that thirst is a gift. It's the first movement of repentance—the realization that you cannot live without Him.

When you wake up before dawn, the world is still. No voices, no food, no distractions—just silence. You stand in a *"desolate"* land, a space not yet shaped by the routines or burdens of the day. Your heart may feel heavy, scattered, or spiritually numb. You haven't yet been warmed by grace. This is the *"waterless"* land within you—the soul that has not yet turned to drink from the presence of God.

The whole day stretches before you, and you don't know what it will bring—what trials, what blessings, what emptiness. For many, the morning feels like entering another dry routine: the same struggles, the same weariness. It can feel lifeless.

But this is where the thirst begins—the moment when you realize that without God, today is just another desert.

When you pray this Psalm, you are choosing to begin your day with reverence, with longing, with a deep seeking of God. You give your first words not to anxiety or distraction, but to Him. You don't just reach for water—you reach for His presence. And you find that this thirst isn't just in the morning—it is always with you, because your soul never stops seeking union with God.

Let your first cry each day be, *"O God, my God."* Let it rise from a heart that thirsts—not in despair, but in hope. For even in the wilderness, He is near.

3. So in the holy place I appear before You, To see Your power and Your glory.

David recalls a time when he stood in the sanctuary of the Lord, the holy place where God's presence dwelled—the Tabernacle, and later the Temple, especially the Holy of Holies, where the Ark of the Covenant was kept. There, in the sacred stillness of worship, David had encountered God's power and glory—not merely through external ritual, but through real communion with the divine.

Now you remember those moments when you stood in the sanctuary of the Lord—in the stillness of prayer, in the beauty of the Divine Liturgy, or in the quiet awe that sometimes fills your heart when God makes Himself known. Like David, you may recall a time when you encountered God's power and glory—not just through outward ritual, but through true communion with the divine presence.

In those sacred moments, you glimpsed something more than symbols. You saw the power of God at work—perhaps not in parted seas or descending fire, but in the deliverance He gave you from fear, in victories over despair, or in the still fire of His grace settling over your soul. You felt His glory—radiant, holy, otherworldly. Not imagination, not emotion, but a foretaste of theosis, a true encounter with His uncreated light.

But now, perhaps you feel far from that place. Like David in the wilderness, you may be waking in the early hours of a new day feeling distant from God, burdened, spiritually dry. You are not in the sanctuary—but the sanctuary is not lost to you. You may be far from the Temple, but you are not far from God. Your soul still remembers His glory, and that memory itself becomes a prayer.

Even if you feel like you are in a wilderness, carry this truth in your heart: you are not exiled from God. You carry the sanctuary within you, for the Holy Spirit dwells in your soul. Turn to Him with a humble and pure heart, and you will reconnect with His glory. You do not need to be in Jerusalem to be in His presence.

Archimandrite Aimilianos writes:

> "O Lord, it is only when our hearts have been separated from the world that we can communicate with You, entering into the divine darkness of Your presence». For the Eternal One does not mingle with the transitory things of time. God is inaccessible to all, yet accessible to the soul, giving Himself to those who turn to Him with their whole heart, and who have the kind of spirit expressed in the following verse."

So rise. Awaken your heart. Give it wholly to God. Seek His power and His glory—not in the noise of the world, but in the silence of your soul.

4. Because Your mercy is better than life, My lips shall praise You.

This verse reveals to you one of the most profound truths in the spiritual life. The word translated as "mercy" is ἔλεος—the same word you cry out in every Orthodox service: "Lord, have mercy" (Κύριε ἐλέησον). This is not a request for mere pity. You are calling upon the life-giving, healing, and redeeming presence of God.

When you pray, "*Your mercy is better than life*," you are making a radical confession: that God's love is more precious than everything else life could give you. Even if you were offered many lives—filled with success, health, comfort, or even beautiful relationships—His mercy would still be greater. To truly know this mercy is to live in communion with God. And that communion is the real life your soul was created for. Without God's mercy, your life remains empty and restless. With it, even the wilderness you walk through becomes holy ground.

The second half of the verse—*"my lips shall praise You"*—is your natural response to such love. When your heart becomes aware of the mercy of God, it cannot stay silent. Your lips become the voice of your soul, not speaking from duty but from an overflowing well of awe, gratitude, and love. This kind of praise does not depend on good circumstances. It rises even in pain, even in loneliness—because you know He is near, and His mercy endures forever.

So when you pray this verse, remember His mercy—not just in thought, but with your whole being. Let your praise become a living response to His love. Bless Him not only with belief, but with your voice, your breath, and your life.

5. Thus I will bless You in my life; I will lift up my hands in Your name.

This verse reveals to you the true purpose of your life: to bless and glorify God continually—not just with words, but with your whole being, in every moment and every action. David shows you what it means to live a life entirely directed toward God—a life of unbroken worship.

The Greek word for *"bless"* (εὐλογέω) means "to speak well"—to speak words filled with truth, mercy, and light. When you bless God, you aren't simply saying something nice; you are aligning your speech with the light of Christ. And more than that, you are living in a way that reflects His presence in you. Blessing God is not something reserved for the church or for moments of formal prayer—it should become the rhythm of your life, the natural expression of a heart that belongs to Him.

So when you say, "*I will bless You in my life,*" you are declaring that as long as you breathe, your life is God's. Your body, your mind, your desires, and your actions all belong to Him. You are choosing to live without division or distraction—gathering your whole self and offering it back to the One who gave it to you.

The second half of the verse—"*I will I lift up my hands in Your name*"—deepens this act of offering. To lift your hands is one of the most ancient gestures of prayer. It is the movement of your soul reaching upward—asking for mercy, praising in thanksgiving, surrendering in trust. It is not a performance; it is your body participating in the longing of your soul. You are saying, with your whole being, "I reach for You, Lord—because nothing else will satisfy me."

In the Church, this gesture is also understood as sacrifice and service—offering your life wholly to God, like a faithful servant who says, "I am Yours." The Fathers even saw this movement in moments of spiritual battle and victory.

Remember Moses, lifting his hands in prayer while Israel fought Amalek (Exodus 17:11). As long as his hands were raised, Israel prevailed. Your raised hands in prayer, lifted in love and persistence, uphold your soul in every trial.

So let this verse shape your life—not just your words, but your direction, your posture, your breath:

> Bless God in everything.
> Lift your hands in longing, thanksgiving, and surrender.
> Live with one aim: to be united with Him.

6. May my soul be filled, as if with marrow and fatness, And my mouth shall sing praise to You with lips filled with rejoicing.

In the world of the ancient Near East, "marrow and fatness" symbolized abundance, richness, and joyful celebration. Marrow—the innermost, most nourishing part of the bone— was considered a luxury, something deeply satisfying. Fatness referred to the choicest portions of the animal, the best cuts reserved for sacrifices and feasts, a sign of blessing, favor, and divine fullness.

When you say, *"May my soul be filled, as if with marrow and fatness,"* you are asking for a satisfaction that goes far beyond physical needs. You are praying for your soul to be filled at the deepest level—spiritually, emotionally, and existentially. This verse gives you a picture of complete contentment, found only in the presence of God.

You know what it means to be hungry for more than food. You've felt the ache in your soul—the thirst that nothing in this world can quench. Just as a rich meal satisfies the body, communion with God satisfies the deepest hunger of your heart. This verse answers the cry you prayed earlier: "My soul thirsts for You in a dry and thirsty land." Now, that thirst is being quenched—not with worldly pleasures, but with the joy and fullness of God's presence.

In the Orthodox tradition, this is the mystery of spiritual nourishment. Your soul is filled with divine grace—through prayer, through stillness, through contemplation, and most fully in the Divine Liturgy and the Holy Eucharist, where you truly "taste and see that the Lord is good."

And when your soul is filled, something beautiful happens: praise begins to overflow. *"Lips filled with rejoicing"* aren't just about fleeting happiness—they express a joy that springs from knowing who God is. Even if you are walking through your own wilderness, even if you're far from comfort or ease, you can rejoice—because God is with you, and in Him, you have enough.

The Fathers remind you that true joy doesn't come from your circumstances—it comes from the presence of God within you. To rejoice in God is to hold a joy that the world cannot give—and cannot take away.

So when you pray this verse, ask that your soul be filled with His goodness. Let your lips become the voice of your joy. Speak not out of duty, but from fullness. Praise Him not just with belief, but with rejoicing—because He is with you, and that is enough.

7. If I remembered You on my bed, I meditated on You at daybreak;

This verse invites you into a deep and personal love for God—a love that stays with you even in the quiet hours of the night. When the world is still and sleep wraps the earth in silence, your heart remains awake. Your thoughts don't need to wander into anxiety, fantasy, or distraction; they can rest in the Lord.

"If I remembered You on my bed:" To remember God on your bed is to turn toward Him in the most unguarded and intimate moments of your day. These are the moments of solitude, silence, and stillness—when no one sees you but God. This is hidden prayer, the kind that doesn't need words. It is communion born from love, where your soul quietly keeps Him present within.

In the Orthodox tradition, this kind of remembrance is treasured. The saints speak often of the importance of your final thoughts before sleep. What your soul holds in the night shapes the heart's interior world. So before you lay your head down, prepare your heart in evening prayer. Let it be your desire through the night to remember Him.

St. John Chrysostom writes:

> "We must always remember God, and especially when our mind is tranquil. If we call God to mind during the day, cares will come rushing in, along with the distractions and the noise of the day, and so the recollection of God is more effective at night, when the soul is tranquil and at rest." (On Hebrews 14:4, PG 63:115)

The second half of the verse—"*I meditated on You at daybreak*"—completes this sacred rhythm. You begin and end your day in God. The early morning hours, known in the Church as Orthros, are not just a time but a spiritual hour—just before sunrise, when light begins to touch the darkness and your soul is most open to grace.

David speaks from experience: his first movement after waking is not toward distraction or routine, but toward God. Let it be the same for you. Let your soul rise first in prayer. The word μελετῶ—"to meditate"—means more than silent thought. It means loving attention, prayerful focus, and often the quiet repetition of God's word, like a sacred rhythm that fills your inner being with light.

The dawn is not just a clock's hour—it is a spiritual awakening. Your soul stirs with the world and turns again to God. In the Orthodox tradition, this is the time set apart for psalmody, for thanksgiving, for offering the first fruits of your day to the Lord.

This verse teaches you that prayer is not merely something you do—it's something you become. David shows you a life shaped by communion, where even resting and waking are acts of worship. Take this rhythm into your own life. Let your soul be framed by evening remembrance and morning meditation. And over time, you will become a vessel of ceaseless prayer, a heart that beats with love for God through every moment of the day and night.

8. For You are my helper, And in the shelter of Your wings I will greatly rejoice.

The language is intimate: "*You are my helper*" reflects a relationship that has grown through trials. David doesn't just hope God will help him—he knows that it is so from his memory, gratitude, and trust in God. He knows it as the help of the One who created him, Who knows the soul's needs better than it does itself. God helps not only by changing circumstances, but by changing the heart, by being with you in all things—including pain and uncertainty.

Archimandrite Aimilianos writes;

> "Those who love God are filled with—that is, they know
> and experience— God's divine power and grace."

Like David you too should have such experiences of God helping you through the trials and tribulations of your daily life.

The phrase, "*in the shelter of Your wings will I greatly rejoice*" expresses this trust, protection, and joy in God's nearness. It evokes the image of a bird sheltering its young under its wings—a recurring and powerful biblical metaphor. For instance, Psalm 90:4–91:4 declares, "He will cover you with his shoulders, and under his wings you will find refuge." In ancient Israelite thought, the image of God's wings pointed to the Ark of the Covenant, where two cherubim spread their wings over the mercy seat—the place where God's presence dwelled (Exodus 25:20). To be under God's wings was to be in His presence, under His mercy, and within His protection.

David is saying that he is safe because God is close to him and he rejoices because he knows from experience that God will cover you, and protect you. Just as a small bird hides under its mother's wing from predators, so the your soul can find peace and joy in the nearness of God.

In the Orthodox tradition, this verse is often prayed during times of spiritual struggle, reminding us that God's presence is our refuge. The "*shelter of Thy wings*" becomes a symbol for:

- The Church, where we are covered by grace
- The Divine Liturgy, where we stand under God's mercy seat The inner stillness where the soul meets God in prayer

When praying this verse, remember how God is your shelter and rejoice in His divine protection. Seek His help for your difficulties and He will show you a way to overcome them.

9. My soul follows close behind You; Your right hand takes hold of me.

This verse beautifully expresses the intimate relationship between your deepest human longing and God's divine grace—between your soul's desire for God and His faithful, loving response. When you say, "*My soul follows close behind You*," you are using a word full of meaning. In Greek, the verb ἐκολλήθη (from κολλάω) means to cling, to stick closely, or to follow with unwavering attachment. It's the same word used in Genesis to describe the bond between husband and wife—total, inseparable union. This is the kind of bond your soul was created for: to hold fast to God in love, trust, and need.

Think of David's situation—alone in the wilderness, pursued, suffering. And yet, his soul clings to God. His desire doesn't come from ease or comfort; it comes from hardship. In the face of danger and abandonment, his instinct is not to run from God, but to draw nearer. So it is with you. Your soul, even when weary or afraid, knows where to turn for life and strength.

The second part of the verse—"*Your right hand takes hold of me*"—completes this picture. In Scripture, the right hand of God represents power, favor, authority, and salvation. It is not distant or indifferent. The verb used here, ἀντελάβου (from ἀντιλαμβάνομαι), means to take hold of, to support, to catch. Picture a father catching a stumbling child before they fall— that is the nature of God's help. Immediate. Personal. Intimate. Like Peter on the water, when you begin to sink, Christ's hand is already there, reaching for you.

Even when you are straining to hold on, it is ultimately God who holds you. That's the mystery at the heart of the Orthodox spiritual life: yes, you strive, you pray, you cling with all your might— but your strength alone is not enough. It is His grace that supports you. His hand upholds you. This verse becomes both your confession of weakness and your testimony of God's faithfulness. Without Him, you would fall. But with His hand upon you, you can endure, rejoice, and rise.

Archimandrite Aimianos writes:

> "For our spiritual lives to bear fruit, two things are necessary: the exercise of our free will, which is expressed in the first part of this verse, and the divine grace, which is expressed in the second."

David doesn't speak of his own strength. What he shows is a heart that simply longs not to be separated from God. The power to remain in union with God comes not from effort alone—but from God Himself.

Saint Athanasios of Alexandria writes:

> "Not even for a moment, my God, candy spirit be separated from You, for I am afire with ardent love, and, as if my mind were a mass of glue, I adhere to You in desire."

So when you pray this verse, recognize the deep desire your soul has to remain united with God. Ask Him to help your free will cooperate with that desire—to not resist, to not delay, to not doubt. And when your heart is turned to Him, He will act—quickly, faithfully, and with the strength that only He can give.

**10. But they seek for my soul in vain;
   They shall go into the lowest parts of the earth.**

**11. They shall be given over to the edge of the sword;
   They shall be a portion for foxes.**

Now you turn your focus to those who rise against you—not just external enemies, but spiritual ones as well. Historically, David spoke of those who pursued his life in the wilderness, especially during Absalom's rebellion, when even his own son sought to take his throne. But this Psalm invites you to see deeper than political or personal conflict. Anyone or anything that tries to separate you from God is, in truth, an enemy of your soul—and therefore an enemy of God.

These enemies may come in many forms: people who harm you, demonic forces that whisper lies, or even inward passions and thoughts that stir fear, pride, despair, or rebellion. They rise up against your calling, your hope, your communion with the Lord. Spiritually, they represent anything that seeks to pull you away from the God you cleave to. But their pursuit is in vain—because your soul clings to God, and His right hand upholds you.

This verse speaks a sobering truth about the fate of those enemies: *"They shall go into the lowest parts of the earth."* This is more than a prediction of physical death—it's a vision of spiritual consequence. The "lowest parts" refer to Sheol, the place of descent, isolation, and separation from the light of God. In Orthodox teaching, this descent is not a punishment imposed by God—it's the path chosen by a soul that turns away from Him. When your soul chooses love, it ascends toward Him; but when it chooses pride, hatred, or the passions, it collapses inward. Evil may seem strong for a time, but its end is always the same: futility, darkness, and ruin.

David continues: *"They shall be given over to the edge of the sword."* This is not about vengeance—it is about divine justice. The words "given over to" implies their fall is not accidental but permitted by God. In Scriptures, the sword is the image of God's justice—of truth that cuts through lies and darkness. It's not your strength that defeats your spiritual enemies, but the sword of God's Word, which the New Testament describes as "living and active, sharper than any two-edged sword" (Hebrews 4:12). When God's truth enters your heart, it cuts down the passions and exposes the enemy's schemes.

Finally, you hear the striking words: "*They shall be a portion for foxes.*" In ancient times, to die unburied, to be consumed by wild animals, was the height of disgrace. Foxes—or jackals—were scavengers, roaming desolate places. To become their portion meant to be forgotten, cast aside, lost to the wasteland.

Spiritually, this image reveals what happens to sin that is never repented of: it devours itself. The passions, if not surrendered to God, consume your soul from within. But the soul that cleaves to God does not end in ruin. It is protected, sustained, and filled with life.

So as you pray this verse, do not fear the enemies that rise against you—whether they are visible or hidden within. Do not doubt God's presence or His power. Whatever darkness you face, no matter how great, God is greater. Pray with love, with thanksgiving, with confidence. Let your soul follow its deep longing to be united with Him. For when you cleave to Him, no enemy can stand. You are upheld by His right hand.

12. But the king shall be glad in God;
  All who swear by Him shall be praised,
  For the mouth that speaks unrighteous
  things is stopped.

This final verse brings you to a place of quiet victory and spiritual clarity. You are reminded that your joy does not come from personal vindication or earthly success, but from God Himself. Even when you feel exiled—misunderstood, pursued, or slandered—you can still rejoice, because your heart remains rooted in the Lord. This gladness is not about your situation changing; it's about your communion with God being restored and unshaken.

You are not alone in this. David, speaking as the king, affirms that all who "shall be glad in God"—all who remain loyal to Him, who confess His name with faith and courage—will be honored. In the biblical world, to swear by God was to publicly declare your covenant with Him. For you, it means to stand firm in faith, even when it's hard, even when no one else sees. And though the world may not recognize it, God and His Church do. You are seen. You are known. You are upheld.

The verse ends with a stark contrast: "*The mouth that speaks unrighteous things.*" Those who accused, slandered, or acted deceitfully will be silenced. Their words—once sharp, once threatening—will lose their power. This is not merely poetic justice; it is the truth revealed. In the end, it is God who will have the final word. The faithful will rejoice. The voices of falsehood will fall silent.

This verse leaves you with a clear choice: cling to God and rejoice, or oppose Him and be silenced. It is a word of hope, of vindication, of encouragement to your soul when you walk through darkness. It tells you: hold on to the light.

So when you pray this final verse, remember the faith and confidence David had in the goodness of God. Don't waver. Don't give in to fear. Trust that God will protect you—as long as you surrender to Him, believing in His mercy, and standing in His strength. Let your joy be in Him. And let your life be a witness that even in exile, even in struggle, the righteous will rejoice.

Summary

As you come to the end of this Psalm, let it remain with you— not only as a prayer you've spoken, but as a way of being you now carry. This is the Psalm of the soul that refuses to let go of

God, even in desolation. It has taught you that thirst is not your enemy, but your invitation. That hunger is not emptiness, but a doorway to communion. That exile from worldly comforts may lead to intimacy with the only One who truly satisfies.

Now you know where to turn in dryness: to the sanctuary of God's presence, even if it is hidden deep within your heart. You know what it means to bless God with your life, to lift up your hands not in routine but in surrender. You've learned that remembrance of God before you sleep and meditation upon Him as you rise will shape the very rhythm of your days.

And above all, you've seen that though your soul may cleave to God with trembling hands, it is His right hand that upholds you.

Let this Psalm become the voice of your mornings, the strength of your trials, the song of your wilderness, and the memory of His mercy. Let it teach you not only how to pray—but how to long, how to cling, how to live.

In the wilderness of each day, may your soul always thirst for Him. And in His mercy, may you always be satisfied.

PSALM 87 (88)

1 An ode of a psalm for the sons of Korah; for the End, for the Mahalath to respond; uderstanding for Heman the Israelite.

2 O Lord God of my salvation, I cry day and night before You.

3 Let my prayer come before You;
Incline Your ear to my supplication, O Lord.

4 For my soul is filled with sorrows,
And my soul draws near to Hades;

5 I am counted among those who go down into the pit;
I am like a helpless man, free among the dead,

6 Like slain men thrown down and sleeping in a grave,
Whom You remember no more,
But they are removed from Your hand.

7 They laid me in the lowest pit,
In dark places and in the shadow of death.

8 Your wrath rested upon me,
And You brought all Your billows over me.
(Pause)

9 You removed my acquaintances far from me;
They made me an abomination among themselves;
I was betrayed, and did not go forth.

10 My eyes weakened from poverty;
O Lord, I cry to You the whole day long;

I spread out my hands to You.

11 Will You work wonders for the dead?
Or will physicians raise them up, and acknowledge You?

12 Shall anyone in the grave describe Your mercy
And Your truth in destruction?

13 Shall Your wonders be known in darkness,
And Your righteousness in a forgotten land?

14 But I cry to You, O Lord,
And in the morning my prayer shall come near to You.

15 Why, O Lord, do You reject my soul,
And turn away Your face from me?

16 I am poor and in troubles from my youth;
But having been exalted, I was humbled and brought into despair.

17 Your fierce anger passed over me,
And Your terrors greatly troubled me;

18 They compassed me like water all the day long;
They surrounded me at once.

19 You removed far from me neighbor and friend,
And my acquaintances because of my misery.

Psalm 87 is one of the darkest and most sorrowful prayers in all of Scripture. This is not a Psalm of deliverance, but a Psalm of raw endurance—a cry from the soul that feels utterly abandoned, yet still chooses to speak to God. You can relate to this as you grasp the reality of your sinfulness and separation from God. Though you may not hear an answer, you are reminded that even in the silence, your cry is not in vain.

This Psalm gives voice to those times when your suffering is overwhelming, when God seems far away, when even your friends have turned from you, and you realize that life in this world has an end and you may be descending into the grave separated from God. And yet, you keep praying. You keep crying out day and night. You lift your hands, even when your strength is gone.

This is the prayer of someone who, though surrounded by darkness, refuses to let go of God. You are not alone in this. The Church gives you this Psalm to read every morning, not to burden you, but to help you embrace your suffering, your separation from God, and your loneliness, knowing these difficulties are not foreign to faith—they are part of the path. And even when the Psalm ends without resolution, your prayer continues.

Let this Psalm become your own cry when words fail. Through it, you learn that God hears even when He seems silent, and that the soul who cries to Him when you feel abandoned by Him is never truly alone.

Commentary:

Psalm 87 is not attributed to David.

1. **An ode of a psalm for the sons of Korah; for the End, for the Mahalath to respond; understanding for Heman the Israelite.**

The sons of Korah were Levitical singers and temple musicians descended from Korah, who (despite their ancestor's rebellion) were reinstated for sacred service. Their attributed Psalms often deal with deep suffering, yearning for God, and the mystery of divine justice.

"For the End:" referring to the end times, death, or the Messianic fulfillment. St. Athanasius and other Fathers see this phrase as Christological: pointing to Christ, the "End" (cf. Romans 10:4– Christ is the end of the law).

"Mahalath" possibly a musical term (name of a melody or tune) or a liturgical instrument or mode

"Heman the Israelite" is one of the wise men of Israel (cf. 1 Kings 4:31), and a Levite musician appointed by David (1 Chronicles 6:33; 15:17–19). This attribution means the Psalm is linked with deep liturgical and musical wisdom, possibly composed or arranged by Heman or in his tradition.

2. O Lord God of my salvation,
   I cry day and night before You.

3. Let my prayer come before You;
   Incline Your ear to my supplication, O Lord.

"*I cry day and night*" becomes your unyielding call to God—a relentless expression of your need for His help. It speaks not only of the depth of your distress but also of a determined faith that refuses to give up hope. Even when you are overwhelmed, your soul continues to reach out for deliverance, trusting that God hears.

When you call Him the "*God of my salvation,*" you are confessing that He alone is your rescuer. This name is more than a title—it is a profession of your trust in His power to save, heal, and restore. In your pain or spiritual struggle, you are reminded that salvation does not come from yourself, or from the world, but from God alone. Even if He seems distant, you must remain steadfast in faith, knowing He is your only true refuge.

When you say, "*Let my prayer come before You,*" you are not speaking into the void. You are lifting your heart before the One who sees and knows all. It is a cry that longs to be heard, to be received, to be embraced by God's mercy. It reflects that your soul cannot bear silence any longer and is pleading to be noticed.

"*Incline Your ear to my supplication*" paints a vivid image—of God stooping down to hear your trembling voice. You are not demanding, but begging with sincerity: "Lord, come closer. Please listen." The word supplication reveals the depth of your struggle. You are exposing the brokenness of your heart, covered with passions, before Christ whom you know to be compassionate. You are appealing to the God you know who listens to those who struggle with sincerity, striving for perfection and now calling out in hope.

This passage teaches you something vital: in your darkest moments, seek God— not with polished words, but with honesty and persistence. He hears you. Even when silence seems to reign, even when the darkness lingers, He is present. You are called to follow the psalmist's example—bring your vulnerability, confess your dependence, and wait with hope. God will answer. In His time. In His way.

But never without love.

4. For my soul is filled with sorrows, And my soul draws near to Hades.

This verse assumes that you have an awareness that your life is fragile and destined to end. Praying this, you are expressing a deep and painful awareness of your condition. You desire to make a plea for God's mercy to break through the shadows that surround your soul. You are not just lamenting; you are reaching out with urgency, asking God to enter your darkness.

"My soul is filled with sorrows." When you say this, you are naming the condition that you recognize in your inner being. These *"sorrows"* are not ordinary sadness but the deep distress that comes when you finally recognize the state of your soul in light of what God expects of you and the limits of this life. You may feel that God is far away. This is what the Fathers call spiritual darkness—a condition not of failure, but of profound trial. Even the most faithful endure such a condition. And you are not alone in this. Remember Christ's cry from the Cross: "My God, My God, why hast Thou forsaken Me?" In that moment, He entered into your own darkness—fully divine, yet embracing the depths of your pain. This is the mystery of divine compassion: God not only understands, He has entered your suffering.

"And my soul draws near to Hades." Hades, the place of the departed, becomes a symbol of that dreadful nearness to separation, isolation, and emptiness when you realize that life is temporary, and the presence of God seems lost in the distance. And yet you are crying out, still hoping to be rescued. In this state, you are not simply lamenting mortality; you are confronting the very boundary between life and death.

But this confrontation can become a holy thing. The Church Fathers often urge you to remember your death—not to terrify you, but to sober you, to awaken you to what is lasting and real. This moment of the Psalm becomes your wrestling with that reality: that life is not forever, and yet God is.

This verse invites you into a deeper honesty. Life brings real suffering, real confusion, and sometimes overwhelming despair.

But God does not reject the brokenhearted. You are allowed—even encouraged—to cry out from that place of sorrow. What matters is that you do not close your heart. Instead, you must open it wide to God, even if all you can offer is a whisper of sorrow. He hears. And it is often in your most desperate moments that the door opens—however slightly—for His mercy to flood in.

**5. I am counted among those who go down into the pit;
I am like a helpless man, free among the dead,**

The "*pit*" you read about in the Psalms is more than just a poetic image—it becomes your own symbol of spiritual darkness. In the ancient world, a pit could be a grave, a prison, or a place of abandonment—a dry well or deep cistern, ten or twenty feet down, cold, dark, and nearly impossible to escape. When you feel trapped in despair or overwhelmed by sorrow, this is the kind of place your soul may seem to inhabit.

When you're in that place, it can feel like you're cut off from everything—cut off from others, from light, from hope, and even from God Himself. You're not the first to feel this way. Joseph was thrown into such a pit. So was the prophet Jeremiah. They were left to sink into mud and silence. The Psalms take that physical reality and reveal its spiritual depth: being cast into the pit means entering the most profound kind of inner suffering—a place where you feel forgotten, forsaken, and alone.

And yet, even from this pit, you cry out.

You may feel as though your soul is slipping into Sheol—the ancient name for the realm of the dead—a shadowy place far from the warmth of God's presence. You may feel abandoned, as if you are "a man without help," utterly alone in your struggle, without anyone to lift you or listen. But even in that darkness, you call out to the Lord. That cry itself becomes your act of faith, however faint. It means you have not given up completely. It means you still long for God to come.

To say you are *"free among the dead"* is to describe the most haunting condition: you are alive in body, but inwardly you feel dead. You still breathe and move, but it's as if your spirit has been loosed into a realm of silence and hopelessness. You are *"free"* not in the joyful sense, but in the sense of being released—let go, abandoned—drifting among those who are no longer aware of suffering. And yet you suffer still, because you are painfully aware of what you've lost: God's nearness, His comfort, His light.

This is what it means to live in a kind of limbo—present in the world, but spiritually cast down into the depths. You are not beyond God's reach, but you feel as though He has hidden Himself. This is one of the most difficult places a soul can endure: not numbness, but the full weight of sorrow, and the piercing awareness that you seem to walk alone.

But do not be ashamed of this place. It is not foreign to the saints. This Psalm prepares you for the times when you too will enter your own pit—when prayer is dry, when suffering isolates you, when the heavens feel silent. These feelings do not mean you are far from God; rather, they are often the very soil in which humility, longing, and deep trust begin to grow. When you find yourself in such darkness, let this Psalm teach you to cry out— not because you feel strong, but precisely because you feel weak.

God hears that cry. He always has.

6. Like slain men thrown down and sleeping in a grave,
Whom You remember no more,
But they are removed from Your hand.

7. They laid me in the lowest pit,
In dark places and in the shadow of death.

When you say, "*Like slain men*," you're not just talking about physical death—you are confessing a feeling of being spiritually lifeless, abandoned, cut off from hope. In the original Hebrew, the word used can mean someone pierced through, like a soldier impaled in battle. You feel like you're lying among the dead, as if life has ended around you. There's no movement, no breath, only stillness and silence. It's not just that you feel close to death—it's that you feel buried beneath its weight, overwhelmed by a sense of God's absence.

This is what it means to feel spiritually forsaken. Without faith in the light Christ brings, this moment would feel final, like you are left in a wasteland of hopelessness. When you're surrounded by what seems like the "bodies of the slain," you feel as though life and meaning have disappeared—only the memory of suffering remains.

When you say, "*Whom You remember no more, and they are removed from Your hand*," you are voicing what may be the deepest pain of all—the feeling that God has forgotten you. You fear He has turned away, that His hand no longer holds you, as though He has released you to fall into darkness. You are still alive, but the pain is so deep that it feels as though God has looked away from your suffering. This is not just sadness—it is the kind of sorrow that strips meaning from your life. To be separated from the One who is life itself is a torment deeper than anything physical.

And now you find yourself in *"the lowest pit"*—a place that feels like the very bottom of existence. There's no light. The air is damp. The walls are cold. You are surrounded by silence and feel utterly forgotten. Spiritually, emotionally, even physically, you have reached a place that seems beyond healing. You may wonder, "Where is God? Is there a way out from this depth?"

The *"dark places"* you find yourself in represent confusion and isolation. You feel lost, uncertain, like you're groping through life without direction. You miss the warmth of God's presence—His guidance, His mercy, His peace. It's as if the light has been turned off, and you are left to wander in the shadows of your own soul. You're not just in the dark—you are the dark. It surrounds you, presses on you, and seems to seep inside.

When you speak of the *"shadow of death,"* you are naming that invisible presence of mortality—the constant reminder that death is near, whether through illness, trauma, grief, or spiritual collapse. That shadow casts itself across your life, weighing you down, whispering that all might be lost. The fear that accompanies this sense of doom is real, and so is the temptation to believe you've been left alone.

But this Psalm, in all its darkness, teaches you something essential: you are allowed to cry out from the pit. You don't have to hide your pain from God. Your feelings of abandonment, confusion, and fear are not signs of faithlessness— they are part of the human condition. And like the psalmist, you must learn to cry out from the depths, not because you feel strong, but because you dare to hope.

Because of your faith in Christ, you know this darkness does not have the final word. His light can reach even into the lowest pit. His mercy can find you even when you feel beyond help. And when you lift your voice from the shadows, however faint it may be, He hears you.

And He will not leave you there.

8. Your wrath rested upon me, And You brought all Your billows over me.

When you say, "*Your wrath rested upon me,*" it can feel as though God's judgment has fallen on you, like a great weight pressing down. In your suffering, you may begin to believe that you are under divine punishment—that perhaps you've done something to deserve this pain. But remember: God does not change. He is always love. This feeling of wrath is not a revelation of who God is, but how you perceive Him in your distress. His justice and mercy are always present, even when hidden behind the storm. What feels like wrath may in fact be the painful process of healing, the discipline that leads to restoration. But in the moment, it is hard to see that. It feels like anger, like distance, like abandonment.

You might find yourself thinking, "Is God angry with me? Have I pushed Him away?" That feeling is part of the human struggle—it's how you wrestle with suffering when you don't yet see the purpose behind it. But even when your emotions cry out in confusion, you must remember: His mercy is never gone, and His love is never withdrawn.

When you say, "*You brought all Your billows over me,*" you are describing the sensation of being swept away by life's storms. These "*billows*" are the towering waves of sorrow, pain, and fear that come one after another, without giving you time to recover. You feel as though you're being tossed in a violent sea, powerless to stop the flood. There's no solid ground, no shelter—just wave after wave of grief, confusion, and loss. The suffering feels relentless. And because you believe in God, it may even feel like He is the one sending the waves.

But even here, in the very center of the storm, you are not alone. God is not far off, watching from a distance. He is in the storm with you—even if unseen. He does not abandon you. What separates you from His presence is not His wrath, but your own sense of despair and confusion. If you open your heart even slightly in the midst of this turmoil, you may catch a glimpse of His mercy, steady and unwavering beneath the waves.

This verse teaches you to be honest about your feelings. It's okay to feel overwhelmed. It's okay to cry out in confusion or to feel like you've been left behind. But don't let that be the end of the story. Keep crying out. Keep seeking. Even in the storm, keep calling on His name.

Because the truth is this: God's love is deeper than any wave that crashes over you. His mercy is wider than the sea. And His hand can reach you, even in the depths.

Remember what St. Porphyrios said:

> "Whoever loves Christ is always joyful, always ready to confront anything. He is fearless." (*Wounded by Love*)

That love—your love for Christ—is the light that will carry you through the storm. When you cling to that love, you will find courage in the very heart of your suffering.

You will find Christ there.

**9. You removed my acquaintances far from me,
They made me an abomination among themselves;
I was betrayed and did not go forth.**

When you say, "*You have removed my acquaintances far from me*," you are naming the painful reality of isolation. It's not just that you are suffering—it's that you feel like you have to suffer alone. The people you once trusted, those who used to check on you or comfort you, may now seem distant, unreachable. And in that distance, you begin to feel not only forgotten but unwanted. No one truly understands what you're going through, and maybe they don't even want to. In your darkest hours, even your closest friends can seem like strangers.

And it doesn't stop there. You might begin to feel as though others see you not with compassion, but with contempt. That's why you say, "*They made me an abomination among themselves*." It's as if your suffering has made you repulsive— unclean, cursed, or marked by some unseen shame. People who once comforted you now seem to turn away. Their silence or suspicion adds a deeper wound. It's not just that you're in pain; it's that you feel forsaken by those who were once your refuge. This is the weight of spiritual isolation—not just separation from others, but from their love, their understanding, their very presence.

You begin to feel "*delivered up*"—as though something, or someone, has allowed you to fall into this suffering. There's a sense of betrayal, or at least abandonment. You didn't choose this, and yet here you are, left in a place where you have no control over your pain. It feels like you've been handed over to sorrow, like a prisoner given into the hands of his jailer.

And now you say, "*I have not come forth*"—because you feel trapped. As if there is no way out. You're stuck in a kind of prison, locked into your pain, unable to move forward or find relief. The darkness becomes a cell. The silence, your only companion. In that place, you are left alone with your thoughts, your guilt, your weariness. You feel stripped of all help, all comfort. There's no one left to turn to. No door seems open.

And yet, even here, there is a lesson.

You are being taught something profound: when the world and even your closest friends fail to understand or support you, your only hope is to reach upward. In this place of inner darkness, you are called to turn not outward, but inward and upward— to seek your healing not from the comforts of the world, but from Christ. The Church is your hospital. The sacraments are the medicine your soul needs. And your spiritual father—he is the one who can walk with you, pray with you, and speak the words of Christ into your darkness.

So don't be afraid of the silence. Let it teach you to listen. Don't be afraid of the darkness. Let it teach you to seek the light. And don't be afraid of being alone— for even in your solitude, Christ is there.

10. My eyes weakened from poverty; from poverty; O Lord, I cry to You the whole day long; I spread out my hands to You

When you say, "*My eyes weakened,*" you are speaking from the depths of exhaustion—where even your ability to see, to understand, to hope, has grown dim. Your eyes, which are meant to perceive light, now feel heavy and blurred from sorrow. You've wept so long that you can barely see anymore. But this is more than physical fatigue; it may be that your spiritual sight has grown weak as well. You no longer perceive God as clearly as you once did. His nearness feels hidden. The joy you once found in Him seems lost, and the light of His presence appears to have faded. You begin to wonder: Is He still with me?

And yet you do not stop there. You cry to Him still.

When you say, *"I cry to You,"* you are affirming that, even in your darkness, even in your exhaustion, God is still the One you seek. You have not turned away from Him. You are not silent. Your voice may be cracked with grief, but it rises up "day and night." You continue to pray, even when you feel no response. You remain turned toward Him, even when all your friends seem far off. He is still the center of your hope—even if that hope is now clothed in tears.

And you spread out your hands.

This gesture—so ancient, so powerful—expresses what words cannot. When you spread out your hands in prayer, you are placing your whole life in God's hands. You are surrendering, reaching, pleading, depending on Him alone. It is a posture of vulnerability and trust. You are not grasping for control—you are asking to be held. Your hands reach upward, not in strength, but in weakness, hoping that He will come and lift you out of this pit.

This is what faith looks like when it is tested. It is not the absence of suffering—it is the refusal to let suffering silence your prayer. You are taught here, through the psalmist's example, that even in your most desperate hours, you must not stop calling out to God. He sees your hands. He hears your cry. And even when He seems far, He is near.

So do not waver. Let your weary eyes look again toward the Lord. Let your tired voice rise one more time in prayer. Stretch out your hands in the darkness. God is not blind. He is not deaf. He is not distant.

He is waiting for your call.

11. Will You work wonders for the dead? Or will physicians raise them up and acknowledge You?

When you say, "*Will You work wonders for the dead?*" you are not questioning God's power—you are crying out from a place of deep despair. You know He can perform miracles. That's not the question. The real question trembling on your lips is this: Will He work a wonder for you, here, in this state where you feel lifeless inside? You feel as though you've already descended into death—not physically, but spiritually. Cut off. Crushed by sorrow. Unable to see the light.

And from that pit, you ask: Can God reach even here? Can His mercy restore someone as lost as I feel right now?

This is not unbelief—it's the cry of a soul standing on the edge of hopelessness, daring to ask for something that seems impossible. But the very act of asking is itself an act of faith. You haven't stopped turning to God. You still believe—dimly, quietly, desperately—that He might hear you. You are still reaching. Still hoping. That's why this verse, though filled with sorrow, also burns with hidden trust. You are saying, Lord, even from this grave, raise me. Make me alive again.

Then you ask, "*Will physicians raise them up?*" And with that question, you admit something painful and freeing: no one on earth can fix what's wrong in your soul. No doctor, no friend, no therapist—however well-meaning or skilled—can truly reach the place where your spirit has collapsed. The wounds you carry go deeper than the body. You've tried to find relief, but now you see it clearly: only God can reach into the heart of this darkness and call life back into being.

In ancient times, the dead were believed to be beyond God's manifest acts of deliverance—they could no longer praise Him, no longer proclaim His mercy. So, you cry out before death overtakes you. You're not only speaking about physical death, but the death of faith, of joy, of nearness to God. You're begging: Act now, Lord. Don't let me slip away into silence. I'm fading. But You alone can restore me.

This moment becomes a turning point. Though your words are filled with sorrow, they reveal your longing—your refusal to give up completely. You are confessing that no human hand can save you. But you believe that God can. Even now. Even here.

So this verse becomes your quiet confession: that only God can bring light where there is no light, hope where all seems lost, and life where you feel dead. And in saying this, you are already opening your heart to Him again.

No matter how far gone you feel, no matter how deep the silence or how heavy the grief, you are never beyond the reach of His mercy.

So cry out. Spread out your hands. He is listening.

12. Shall anyone in the grave describe Your mercy, And Your truth in destruction?

When you say, "*Shall anyone in the grave describe Your mercy?*" you are voicing the fear that death might cut you off not only from life, but from God Himself. It's not that you doubt God's mercy—you fear you may never again live to proclaim it. This cry comes from desperation, from the feeling that if God does not act soon, your opportunity to witness His goodness will vanish into silence. You fear the grave as a place where praise is silenced, where communion is broken, and where the story of God's mercy goes untold.

In the psalmist's time, this fear was not imagined. Sheol—the grave—was seen as a shadowy realm of stillness, where even the righteous were believed to be separated from the community of the living and the worship of God.

Recognizing the reality of life, you now feel that fear echoing through your own pain: If I fall into spiritual death now, if my suffering crushes me before You answer, will I ever again be able to bear witness to Your love?

But here is the good news: your fear is not the end of the story.

Christ has come. He entered even death itself. In Him, the grave is no longer a place of silence—it has become a place touched by mercy. When Christ descended into Hades, He brought light into the darkness, life into the land of the dead. He trampled down death by death, not just symbolically, but truly.

Because of this, your fear of being forever cut off is answered by the most profound truth: you are never beyond the reach of God's love.

Now, when you cry out from your own darkness, when you feel like you've entered a living grave, you are not abandoned. Christ has already gone before you. He has filled even the silence of death with His presence. You are not alone.

This is why the Church prays for the departed—not because we control their fate, but because we know that love does not end at the grave. We remain united with them in Christ. Death is not the end; it is a threshold. And those who fall asleep in the Lord are still held in His mercy. What once was a place of abandonment has become a hidden place of communion.

When you ask, "*And Your truth in destruction?*" you are pleading with Him to act, to show His faithfulness now, to fulfill what He has promised. You are crying out, "Lord, don't let Your name be forgotten in my suffering. If I fall, who will praise You?" This cry becomes part of your faith, not your doubt. It means you still care about God's honor. It means you long to be among the living who glorify Him.

Elder Aimilianos once explained this plea like this:

> "Do You understand that, in order for Your honor to remain untarnished in the world, and for people to place their trust in You, I must be saved?"

You are not asking for comfort only—you are asking that your salvation become a testimony of God's truth and mercy in the eyes of others.

As a Christian, you now live in the light of the Resurrection. You no longer should fear death as the psalmist once did. You know that Christ has destroyed its power. You know that even in your lowest moments, even when you feel buried in sorrow or despair, the love of God still holds you.

So when you pray these verses now, you do so with reverence—but also with hope. Yes, the psalmist's fear was real. But in Christ, the grave is no longer the end. It has become the door to life.

St. Paul says,

> "For I am persuaded that neither death nor life…nor anything else in all creation will be able to separate us from the love of God which is in Christ Jesus our Lord." (Romans 8:38–39)

Let that truth steady your heart. Even in the darkest depths, you are still within the reach of God's mercy.

13. Shall Your wonders be known in darkness, And Your righteousness in a forgotten land?

When you say, *"Shall Your wonders be known in darkness?"* you are crying from a place of affliction, confusion, and deep spiritual pain. You are not questioning whether God can act—you are pleading for Him to act now, in the middle of your darkness. You feel trapped in sorrow and silence, unable to see God's hand, and your heart cries out: "Where are You, my God? Will You show me Your wonders even here, in this shadowed place where I feel so alone?"

This darkness you feel is not just emotional—it has spiritual depth. The Orthodox Church teaches that such darkness, though painful, can be part of your journey toward God. The Fathers do not always treat it as a punishment or a sign of God's rejection, but as a mysterious gift—a stage in your purification. You are being drawn, painfully but lovingly, away from surface-level faith and into deeper communion with the living God.

St. John of the Cross called this the "dark night of the soul." Elder Aimilianos of Simonopetra described it as a burning away of all pride, all false comforts, all illusions of control. When God withdraws the felt sense of His grace, it is like a purifying fire—not to destroy you, but to reveal what in you is real. In this darkness, you are not being abandoned. You are being emptied of everything that keeps you from fully receiving Him.

So your question becomes something more than a cry for help. It becomes a longing: Lord, reveal Yourself, even here. Let this darkness become the place where I come to know You more truly, where my soul is stripped bare and open to Your light.

When you speak of "*Your righteousness*," you are reaching out for more than deliverance. You are asking God to restore what feels lost—His justice, His truth, His covenant love. You are saying, "Lord, You are faithful. I do not see it now, but I believe it still. Come, show me that Your mercy endures, even here in the shadow."

And when you describe this as a "*forgotten land*," you are giving voice to a fear that many souls have known: the fear of being abandoned, of being exiled from God's presence. You feel as though you are in a land where no one remembers, where your prayers echo but do not return. This land is not on any map—it is the interior wilderness of spiritual desolation, the feeling that you are far from both God and others.

But take heart—because Christ has entered even that land.

What once was forgotten is now remembered. Christ descended into Hades not as a victim, but as a conqueror. He shattered the silence of Sheol. He filled the grave with light. You may feel like you've been cast into a place of silence—but He is already there.

You may feel like you've been cut off—but in truth, you are being held. You are not lost. You are not beyond His reach.

So when you cry out, *"Shall your wonders be known in darkness?"*—you are praying with the very voice of faith. Because yes, He will. Even in the darkness, His mercy can be revealed. Even in your most forgotten places, He remembers you. In Christ, what once was a place of silence becomes a place of communion. What once was feared has now become a place of hope.

Keep crying out. Keep longing. Keep seeking. This darkness is not forever. And when the dawn comes, you will know—not only that God has saved you, but that He was with you even in the night.

14. I cry to You, O Lord, And in the morning my prayer shall come near to You.

"I cry to You, O Lord": Here, the psalmist continues to demonstrate his trust in God, confident that God will eventually save him from his condition. He remains hopeful that God will deliver him from his discomfort, especially in the morning when his prayer is strongest and he experiences moments of renewed hope.

"In the morning my prayer shall come near to You": Morning, as the dawn of a new day, carries deep spiritual symbolism. It signifies renewal, hope, and the beginning of new life. Just as the rising sun dispels the darkness of night, so too does it reflect the soul's longing for God's light to overcome the shadows of suffering, confusion, or despair. The psalmist turns to God at the break of day, seeking His mercy, presence, and strength for whatever lies ahead. Morning becomes not just a time of routine,

but a moment of sacred offering, where the soul reaches out to God with expectation and trust.

In ancient Israel, morning was also the appointed time for offering sacrifices, including the daily burnt offering and peace offerings (see Leviticus 7:11, Numbers 28:1–8). This gives deeper context to the psalmist's words: his prayer is like a sacrifice offered at the altar, an expression of faith and devotion at the very start of the day.

Morning prayer, in this sense, reflects a spiritual discipline of putting God first— dedicating the day to Him before any distractions or responsibilities take hold. It becomes an act of surrender and openness to God's will, inviting His grace to shape and sanctify the day from its first moments.

In Orthodox Christian practice, this is beautifully embodied in the Orthros (Matins) service, part of the Church's daily cycle of prayer. These liturgical Hours create a rhythm that sanctifies time itself, helping believers remain rooted in God's presence throughout the day. Morning prayer is not just the beginning of a schedule—it is the beginning of communion, of remembering who we are before God, and of placing our trust in Him anew each day.

This reminds us that beginning the day with God in prayer helps to center our hearts and minds on Him, grounding us in His presence from the very start. Even when life feels overwhelming, setting aside time in the morning for prayer can renew our sense of connection with God, providing the strength, clarity, and peace needed to face the challenges of the day.

15. Why, O Lord, do You reject my soul
And turn away Your face from me?

In biblical language, "*Your face*" often symbolizes God's presence, favor, and attentive love. To see God's face is to experience communion with Him, to be in the light of His grace. So when the psalmist laments, "*Why do You turn away Your face from me?*" he is expressing a profound sense of divine absence—a feeling that God's favor has been withdrawn and that he has been left alone in his suffering. It is the sorrow of a heart that longs for God but perceives only silence.

The phrase "*You reject my soul*" deepens this lament. In the Orthodox tradition, the soul is understood as the immortal and spiritual center of the human person, created in the image of God and made for communion with Him. To feel as though one's soul has been rejected is to experience not only suffering but spiritual abandonment—as if even one's deepest self has been rejected or forgotten by God. This is not a statement of theological fact—God never ceases to love—but a cry from the depths of human pain, where it feels as though even God's love is unreachable.

And yet, even in this desolation, the psalmist's yearning for God remains. His cry is not one of anger, but of desperate hope—a plea for reassurance, for restoration, for the return of divine presence. His longing itself is a form of faith. Even when God feels far, the psalmist does not turn away but continues to call upon Him. This verse teaches us that even when we feel abandoned, our desire for God can become the very bridge back to Him—a cry that draws His mercy near.

16 I am poor and in troubles from my youth;
But having been exalted, I was humbled
and brought into despair.

"I am poor": The term "poor" here may refer not only to material poverty but also to a feeling of being spiritually impoverished, lacking the God's presence for strength, comfort, or resources to cope with life's challenges. The psalmist recognizes a need for God's mercy, acknowledging he is without the means to help.

"In troubles from my youth": This part reflects the psalmist's long-standing experience of hardship. It suggests that from an early age, the psalmist has faced difficulties, adversity, or suffering. This highlights how persistent and enduring hardship can be throughout one's life, and the cumulative effect it has on a person's spirit.

"But having been exalted, I was humbled and brought into despair": This phrase describes the psalmist's experience of having been tossed in the waves of life, possibly a position of honor or success, only to be brought low—humbled and subjected to great difficulty or suffering. It speaks to the dramatic reversal of fortune the psalmist has experienced. This contrast underscores the volatility of life and the fleeting nature of worldly success or honor, as well as the awareness of God's presence. This theme of reversals is common in biblical literature, where individuals are often brought low to learn humility, dependence on God, and the transient nature of earthly status and wealth.

This is a common theme found thoughout the New Testament. The ultimate reversal is seen in Jesus Himself, who descended into the depths of human suffering and death in order to raise humanity into life:

"Though He was in the form of God… He emptied Himself, taking the form of a servant… He humbled Himself, becoming obedient to the point of death, even death on a cross. Therefore, God also highly exalted Him…" (Philippians 2:6–9)

The humiliation of the Cross leads to the glory of the Resurrection. Christ enters despair, abandonment ("My God, My God, why have You forsaken Me?" — Matthew 27:46), and even death, in order to reverse it all—lifting up the fallen and breaking the power of despair itself.

In the Beatitudes (Matthew 5:3–12), Christ blesses those whom the world sees as weak, broken, or despairing:

"Blessed are the poor in spirit…"
"Blessed are those who mourn…"
"Blessed are those who are persecuted…"

Each beatitude is a paradox—a reversal—where what looks like despair or loss becomes the doorway to the Kingdom of Heaven. God's grace is revealed precisely where human strength has failed.

Paul frequently describes his own life and ministry in terms of being brought low, only to be sustained and lifted by God:

"We are afflicted in every way, but not crushed; perplexed, but not driven to despair… always carrying in the body the death of Jesus, so that the life of Jesus may also be manifested in our bodies." (2 Corinthians 4:8–10)

This dynamic of suffering leading to glory is foundational to Paul's theology: it is through weakness that God's power is made perfect." (2 Corinthians 12:9)

Many of Christ's parables center around unexpected reversals:

- The Prodigal Son (Luke 15): from rebellion and despair to forgiveness and restoration.

- The Rich Man and Lazarus (Luke 16): the poor man is exalted; the rich man is cast down.

- The Last Shall Be First (Matthew 20:16): the entire structure of worldly status is inverted.

The New Testament teaches that being brought into despair is not the end, but often the beginning of true spiritual transformation. Just as Christ descended into the darkness of the tomb to rise again in glory, so the believer—when humbled or tested—may be prepared for divine healing, growth, and resurrection. The theme of reversal is a testimony to God's mercy: He raises the lowly, restores the broken, and brings light from the deepest darkness.

This verse should remind us that suffering—especially when it is long and humbling—is not a sign that God has rejected us, but a call to trust more deeply in Him. Life's reversals remind us that we are not in control, and that our true security lies not in success or comfort, but in God's enduring mercy. Even in our poverty and distress, we are not forgotten—our cries are known to God, and in His time, He will raise us up.

17. Your fierce anger passed over me, And Your terrors greatly troubled me.

"Fierce anger" is the psalmist's way of expressing the overwhelming feeling that he is under God's wrath, punishment or anger. Yet in Orthodox understanding, God is always love, light, and life. He does not alternate between loving and being angry. Rather, when we turn away from His love—through sin, pride,

hatred, or the hardening of our hearts—we experience that same unchanging love as pain, correction, or judgment. This is what Scripture often refers to as God's wrath or fury: not a change in God, but the soul's painful experience of love when it is out of harmony with Him.

In such a state, a person may begin to think God is unjust, or even cruel, like a weak child being toyed with. But this is not reality—it is the distorted perception of a soul in anguish.

When we encounter deep spiritual suffering, we are faced with a choice: either to reject it, and be consumed by bitterness and darkness, or to accept it as a mystery allowed by God for our healing. If we choose the path of acceptance, we begin to search for the purpose God intends through the suffering. This can lead to a quiet spiritual transformation, in which God's Kingdom and His love become visible again. But if we refuse this path, the anguish continues, and the sense of abandonment deepens.

Aimilianos comments:

> "It follows from this that the psalmist's salvation hinges on a single decision, namely, the acceptance or rejection of his suffering…If he chooses to entrust himself to God, and so recognize in his suffering God's mercy and love; if he is able to see his suffering as the proof of God's love for him, then he will undergo another transformation to the core of his being. Just when he thinks life is about to end, that he is about to breathe his last breath, he will feel, not simply an upward surge into something new, but deep within himself the presence of the long-lived seed mentioned by the Prophet Isaiah: 'It was the will of the Lord to bruise him; He has put him to grief; yet when he makes himself an offering for sin,

he shall see his offspring, a long-lived seed... he shall see the fruit of the suffering of his soul and be satisfied' (Isaiah 53:10).Spiritual health is not found in the avoidance of suffering, but in its joyful acceptance. The psalmist's dilemma lies precisely in whether or not he will accept his suffering—or reject it—which is another way of saying whether he will accept or deny God."

This is echoed in Matthew 14, when the disciples were in a boat, tossed by waves and fearful for their lives. St. Matthew writes:

"Jesus went to them, walking on the sea. And when the disciples saw Him walking on the sea, they were troubled, saying, 'It is a ghost!' And they cried out for fear. But immediately Jesus spoke to them, saying, 'Be of good cheer! It is I; do not be afraid.'" (Matt. 14:25–27)

Christ was telling them that He is the God of their salvation, and that even the stormy sea can be walked upon calmly if they trust in Him.

This brings us to a crucial spiritual question: when we suffer like this, will we offer ourselves as a sacrifice to the will of God—or not?

St. Macarius the Great, reflecting on the sacrificial system of the Old Testament, writes:

"Similarly also, our soul must approach Christ the High Priest to be slain by Him and die to its own wicked thoughts and the wicked life which it was living—that is, to die to sin. Just as the body, after the soul has left it, is dead and no longer has life in it, so after Christ,

the Heavenly High Priest, puts to death our life in the world, it dies to the life of corruption it formerly lived."
(Spiritual Homilies 1.6, trans. G. Maloney)

True spiritual health is not found in avoiding suffering, but in receiving it with faith and—even—joy, knowing that God, in His love, allows it for our purification, our humility, and ultimately, our transformation.

18. They compassed me like water all the day long. They surrounded me at once.

19. You removed afar from me neighbor and friend, And my acquaintances because of my misery.

This Psalm seems to end without any sense of redemption. Aimilianos suggests that this is due to the way Psalms are traditionally read in sequence, the next Psalm (88, 89) offers the completion to this one.

In the liturgical use of this Psalm the first two verses are repeated:

> 1. Lord God of my salvation, by day have I cried and by night before Thee.

> 2. Let my prayer come before Thee, bow down Thine ear unto my supplication

This closes the Psalm with a hopeful conclusion.

A Concluding Thought:

> "We have considered this Psalm as if it were the expression of the psalmist, but in fact the story is the story of every soul. The tragedy of his dilemma, is some-

thing that we all confront. This is why even a soul that lives within the Church is required to read or hear this Psalm every morning, and not simply read it or hear it, but to experience it just as the psalmist did."
—Archimandrite Aimilianos

Some Key Lessons:

Persistence in Prayer: Even when feeling forsaken, we are encouraged to persist in prayer, trusting in God's salvation.

Acknowledging Suffering: It is natural to feel overwhelmed and abandoned during suffering, and we are encouraged to acknowledge these feelings honestly before God.

Trust in God's Mercy: Despite feelings of rejection and desolation, we are called to trust in God's mercy, even when it feels distant.

Spiritual Transformation Through Suffering: Suffering is a transformative journey that, when accepted, can lead to deeper dependence on God and understanding of His love.

The Importance of Hope: While the Psalm expresses deep despair, it points toward the ultimate hope that God's faithfulness and deliverance will come, even when it is not immediately apparent.

A Choice: We all face a choice to face our suffering and our choice impacts ur salvation. We must choose to accept and embrace it as the love of God. Otherwise we will never overcome it.

Questions for your reflection:

1. In times of distress, do you find yourself consistently crying out to God, even when it feels like He is distant or unresponsive? What does persistent prayer look like in your own life?

2. The psalmist describes feeling overwhelmed and spiritually forsaken. How do you respond when you feel abandoned by God or when it seems like your suffering has no end? How can this Psalm guide you in those moments of despair?

3. The psalmist speaks of being surrounded by "the bodies of the slain" and feeling spiritually dead. Have you ever experienced a time when you felt spiritually disconnected or far from God? What steps can you take to reconnect with God during such times?

4. In what ways do you experience spiritual or emotional isolation during difficult times? Who are the people in your life that help you through such periods, and how can you rely on God's presence when human support seems absent?

5. The psalmist feels like they are drowning in suffering, and their friends have distanced themselves. How do you respond to the pain of others who may feel abandoned or rejected? How can you be a source of comfort and support to those in distress?

6. When suffering feels overwhelming, the psalmist questions whether God can work wonders. How does the idea of God working in the midst of suffering impact your

own perspective on trials? Do you trust that God can bring about transformation, even in your most hopeless moments?

7. The Psalm ends with the psalmist still reaching out to God. How does this persistence in prayer and hope speak to you? When facing challenges, how can you continue to reach out to God, even when answers seem delayed or difficult to perceive?

8. The psalmist reflects on their past struggles and asks for God's mercy. How do you view the times in your life when you have faced personal trials? How might these past struggles lead to a deeper understanding of God's mercy and faithfulness?

* The names Kore, Mahalath, and AHemon (or Lemon) in the superscriptions of Psalms refer to musical or liturgical directions, rather than individuals or specific historical figures.

Korah: This name is associated with a group of Levites who were descendants of Korah (or Kore), the famous Levite mentioned in the book of Numbers. In the context of the Psalms, "the sons of Korah" were a group of Levites known for their musical role in the temple. They were temple musicians and singers, and many Psalms are attributed to them or associated with them, especially in the titles of Psalms like Psalm 42–49, 84, 85, and 87.

Mahalath: This term likely refers to a specific musical or liturgical mode or instrument capable of deep mournful sounds. It may denote a particular melody or style used for the Psalm's performance. In some translations or manuscripts, Mahalath might also be interpreted as a term related to the musical setting or mode rather than an individual.

AHemon: This name is often linked to Hemon (or Aemon), and in some contexts, it might be a reference to an individual musician or a liturgical leader, or it could simply be another musical direction. Some scholars suggest that this could refer to a particular musical arrangement used during the Psalm's performance.

"The end" indicates that this Psalm points to the end of the period of the Old Testament, anticipating the birth of Christ or His Second Coming, a manifestation of God in time,

The phrase "for giving wise instruction" indicates this is a gift of divine grew. This means we should expect to find depths of spiritual understanding. to grasp this Psalm's meaning requires a mature heart that has been cultivated by God's grace, one who has been given the gift of divine understanding. It means that one must go beyond the literal meaning of its words.

PSALM 102 (103)

*1 By David.**
Bless the Lord, O my soul,
And everything within me, bless His holy name.

2 Bless the Lord, O my soul, And forget not all His rewards:

3 Who is merciful to all your transgressions,
Who heals all your diseases,

4 Who redeems your life from corruption,
Who crowns you with mercy and compassion,

5 Who satisfies your desire with good things;
And your youth is renewed like the eagle's.

6 The Lord shows mercies
And judgment to all who are wronged.

7 He made known His ways to Moses,
The things He willed to the sons of Israel.

8 The Lord is compassionate and merciful,
Slow to anger, and abounding in mercy.

9 He will not become angry to the end,
Nor will He be wrathful forever;

10 He did not deal with us according to our sins,
Nor reward us according to our transgressions;

11 For according to the height of heaven from earth,
So the Lord reigns in mercy over those who fear Him;

12 As far as the east is from the west,
So He removes our transgressions from us.

13 As a father has compassion on his children,
So the Lord has compassion on those who fear Him,

14 For He knows how He formed us;
He remembers we are dust.

15 As for man, his days are like grass,
As a flower of the field, so he flourishes;

16 For the wind passes through it, and it shall not remain;
And it shall no longer know its place.

17 But the mercy of the Lord is from age to age upon those who
fear Him, And His righteousness upon children's children,

18 To such as keep His covenant
And remember His commandments, to do them.

19 The Lord prepared His throne in heaven,
And His Kingdom rules over all.

20 Bless the Lord, all you His angels,
Mighty in strength, who do His word,
So as to hear the voice of His words.

21 Bless the Lord, all you His hosts,
His ministers who do His will;

22 Bless the Lord, all His works,
In all places of His dominion;
Bless the Lord, O my soul.

Commentary

In today's world, you—like most of us—have been taught to see life as material, disconnected, and governed by chance. The universe is often presented as indifferent, human existence as accidental, and suffering as something purely unfortunate—without higher purpose or redemption. In this view, meaning is self-made, and praise seems naïve, even irrational. But the Psalms—and Psalm 102 in particular—were not written in such a world. They come from a different vision of reality, one where everything is grounded in divine presence, and where even pain can be transformed by mercy.

This Psalm speaks from a reality where God is never absent, but always present; where mercy is more enduring than punishment; where your soul is not forgotten dust, but something known, crowned, healed, and renewed. This is the world the Orthodox Church calls sacramental—not just in terms of liturgical rites, but in the deeper sense that everything is sacred, and everything has the potential to reveal the presence of God. This is the view of the Apostles.

To read this Psalm with understanding is to enter it, not just to study it. Let it reshape how you see God, how you see the world, and how you understand your own pain and struggles. Psalm 102 teaches you that nothing in your life is wasted. Not even your weakness. Not even your wounds. These too can become praise. These too can be touched by divine mercy.

This commentary is to open it for you—to help you hear its rhythm, feel its depth, and maybe, by the end, even see differently. The psalmist is not giving you an escape from the realities of life— he is showing you the path into a deeper kind of life. A life rooted in communion, in healing, and in love with God.

So enter into this Psalm with your whole heart. Bring your questions, your longing, your tiredness. and your wounds—especially your wounds. And let your soul learn how to say with love: "Bless the Lord, O my soul."

1. By David.

Bless the Lord, O my soul,
And everything within me, bless His holy name.

When David cries out, "*Bless the Lord, O my soul,*" he is not merely reciting words—he is calling from the deepest part of his being to praise and remember God. It is a cry of love, not just of duty. Do not think of this as an intellectual idea or a thought disconnected from your heart; it is the awakening of your soul, rising above the pull of worldly distractions and bodily concerns. Like David, you are expressing a lived reality—that God is present, here and now, in all things. You are saying that your heart is open to a truth greater than what you can see or touch.

In our Orthodox life, we say "Bless the Lord" constantly—in the Divine Liturgy, at Vespers, and in our personal prayers. But this must never become just a habit or a phrase we repeat without thought. It is meant to come from the heart, filled with love, reverence, and awe. Every time you say "Bless the Lord," you are expressing a desire to enter into communion, to awaken your soul and lift it toward God who gives you life.

One of the most common—and most subtle—dangers in the spiritual life is saying holy words while our hearts remain far away. We may speak of God, angels, mercy, and blessing, yet inwardly doubt the reality of spiritual things, reducing them to mere ideas or metaphors. Instead of praying from the heart, we slip into thinking only in philosophical or intellectual terms, disconnected from the living presence of God. But prayers using words like *"Bless the Lord,"* are not meant to be abstract reflections—they are meant to be real encounters with the God who is present, who hears, and who responds.

Jesus warns us of this:

> "These people draw near to Me with their mouth, but their hearts are far from Me." (Isaiah 29:13, quoted by Christ in Matthew 15:8)

You can go through the motions—sing the hymns, read the Psalms, say the words—but if you lack sincerity, are distracted, self-focused, or indifferent, your words don't rise from a loving soul.

You must be watchful when you bless the Lord while your heart is clouded by sin, where praise may rise from your lips, yet pride, resentment, or unforgiveness cling to your soul. It is entirely possible for you to speak holy words while inwardly resisting the very healing reality they summon you into. But true blessing does not require a perfect heart—it comes when your heart is open to spiritual reality, willing to let go, to repent, and to be transformed. To bless the Lord while refusing to acknowledge your sinfulness is to praise superficially. As St. Isaac the Syrian says:

> "The praise that rises from a proud heart becomes noise before God."

Even if you fall into these errors, you can simply recognize the power and presence of His reality, and ask for His help with honesty of heart: "Lord, I bless You—not perfectly, but truly. Help my heart catch up with my words." This kind of prayer is not weakness—it is the beginning of healing. God meets you not in your perfection, but in your sincerity. He receives even your smallest efforts when they are offered in love.

Elder Aimilianos says that to bless the Lord is to acknowledge His beauty, His goodness, His mercy—and to rejoice in it. We're not offering Him something He lacks. We're not saying, "Here's my blessing, God—I hope You like it." We're saying, "Lord, I see You are already full of glory and goodness—and my heart can't help but rejoice in that!"

You don't need perfect words to bless the Lord. You'll know you are truly blessing Him when your prayer comes from a place of recognition, gratitude, sincerity, and love—even if it's small. When your heart simply says, "Thank You, Lord... I trust You... I need You... I praise You," even quietly, even imperfectly—that is blessing the Lord. It's not about eloquence, but about turning your heart toward Him, and offering what you have in truth.

Don't expect or seek emotional feelings. St. Theophan the Recluse reminds us this is not about emotional feelings:

> "Do not be disturbed if you do not feel warmth or tears during prayer... Offer God your faithfulness. Feelings will come in time, if He wills."

That means that even dry, tired prayer can be real and holy—as long as it's sincere.

To "*bless the Lord*" is also a spiritual discipline, a way to train your soul to turn toward God in all circumstances. It can teach you to lift your eyes beyond the material, beyond your immediate struggles, and recognize His presence even in suffering. It's not something you do only when life is easy—it's something you learn to do especially when life is hard. In this way, blessing the Lord becomes a way of anchoring your heart in Him, no matter what you face.

Here are some simple ways to make *"Bless the Lord"* a living part of your life:

> **Morning**: Start your morning by saying it aloud. Before you check your phone, before your mind races with daily tasks — say: *"Bless the Lord, O my soul, and all that is within me, bless His holy name."* This is a way of claiming the day for God, telling your soul: "Wake up, remember, and praise Him."

> **Day time**: When you're stressed, irritated, discouraged, or tempted to complain during the day—quietly say: *"Bless the Lord..."* It doesn't have to be loud or emotional. Just true. This is training. Like lifting spiritual weights: "I bless You even now. I trust You even now."

> **Night**: Every night, write down or quietly name three things you're thankful for—and bless the Lord for them. This teaches your soul to see God is in your life, even on hard days. Repeat this verse, *"Bless the Lord, O my soul..."* This is Eucharistic living—thanksgiving as a way of being.

You're not alone when you say, *"Bless the Lord."* Even if you feel small, uncertain, or unworthy, your voice is joining something much bigger—a living song that began long before you and will continue long after. This Psalm ends by sweeping you into that great mystery: *"Bless the Lord, all His angels... all His hosts... all His works... Bless the Lord, O my soul."* It's as if heaven and earth are singing together—and somehow, you and I are included. Struggling, imperfect, ordinary as we are, we're invited into a symphony of praise that never stops. That's the beauty of it: our little voices matter. They are heard. And they belong to something eternal.

Saying *"O my soul"* implies that you know your soul. You don't often think about your soul or even realize it's there. When David speaks to his soul, he's speaking to everything inside of him: his thoughts, his desires, his will, his memories, his joy, and even his pain. He's calling all of it to turn toward God. He's saying, "All of me, bless Him. Every part—the strong, the weak, the tired, the longing—bless the Lord." It's a prayer that gathers your whole person, not just the part of you that feels spiritual, but even the parts that feel worn out or unworthy Nothing is left out. This is why David adds *"and everything within me."*

In Orthodox teaching, the soul is not a detached spirit, but united with the body in sacred harmony. It is the very core of who you are—created in the image of God and capable of love, freedom, and beauty. The Church Fathers teach that your soul has different powers: a mind that contemplates God, a will that chooses Him, a desire that longs for Him, and the courage to struggle for the good He commands. So when you pray like David, *"Bless the Lord, O my soul,"* you are calling all those inner powers to turn toward God—like flowers turning toward the sun, drawn to His light, warmed by His mercy.

St. Gregory of Nyssa says the soul bears "the imprint of divine beauty." That means your soul is capable of reflecting God through your love, your prayer, your faithfulness. Even when you feel small or unworthy, this is still true. As David reminds us that your blessing the Lord must begin from inside you. It's not just about what you say—it's about how you remember Him, how you give thanks, how you offer your heart to Him, how you express your love for Him.

So when you say, *"bless His holy name,"* you are drawing near to the living God. The God who heals, forgives, restores, and never leaves. To speak His name with reverence is to stand in His light, is to open your heart to the One who is always present, always loving, always reaching toward you. You are not thinking that the name of God is just a word or an idea floating in the air. The name of God is not a term to be defined in a dictionary; it is His presence, His power, His nearness. St. John of Damascus wrote,

> "The name of God is the manifestation of what He is."

In Holy Scripture, a name isn't just a label but it carries the essence and presence of the one named. In Exodus 3:14, when Moses asks God His name, God replies: "I AM WHO I AM." (Hebrew: Ehyeh Asher Ehyeh) This Name—I AM—reveals that God is an eternal, unchanging, absolute being. He depends on no one, but all things depend on Him. The Jews held this Name (Yahweh or Jehovah) in such awe that they would never pronounce it aloud—instead, they said Adonai ("Lord") out of reverence.

In the New Testament, the fullness of God's Name is revealed in Jesus Christ.

> "You shall call His name Jesus, for He will save His people from their sins." (Matthew 1:21)

> "At the name of Jesus, every knee shall bow..." (Philippians 2:10)

When you say the name Jesus, you are not speaking of a person like yourself—you are calling upon God Himself, God's mercy made flesh. To bless the Name of the Lord is to bless Jesus Himself—the Incarnate God, in whom all the love, power, and holiness of God are made visible. In His Name, heaven touches earth, and the fullness of divine mercy comes close enough to be embraced.

To bless the Lord is not a performance, like greeting a good friend, nor is it a routine phrase you simply repeat. These words imply a relationship with the Divine—a movement of your soul that remembers how good God is, and says yes to Him again. It must be more than a mental act. It is what you were made for. And when your soul says with sincerity, *"Bless the Lord,"* all of heaven listens—and your heart becomes a living altar, kindled with the fire of His love.

2. Bless the Lord, O my soul, And forget not all His rewards:

Emphasizing the importance of this blessing, he repeats it adding, *"Forget not all His rewards."* Here he is calling to remembrance—not just of God's gifts, but of His mercy, healing, and salvation. If you forget God's benefits you act as if you are ungrateful, self-reliant, and separated from God.

What are these *"rewards"* or *"benefits"* we must not forget? The Greek word here is ἀνταποδόσεις (antapodoseis), which can be translated as recompenses, returns, or gracious dealings. It implies both: What God has already done (forgiveness, protection, providence). What He continues to do (sustain, heal, restore).

St. Augustine writes:

> "You do not repay Him—He repays you. And with what? With forgiveness, healing, redemption, a crown, and every good thing." (Exposition on Psalm 102)

Elder Aimilianos says,

> "These gifts are God's grace, and grace means something that is free."

Forgetting God's blessings leads you to a cold, lifeless, more intellectual relationship with Him, lacking intimacy and love. By contrast, remembering all He gives you, warms your soul and brings it to bless the Lord even in suffering. The saints practiced this constantly—many even kept a personal list of the mercies they experienced to remember them in prayer.

Saint Porphyrios suffered for years from painful illnesses, including cancer, blindness, and serious respiratory issues. Yet he constantly blessed the Lord and radiated joy. He says:

> "Whatever God allows, I accept with love. I glorify Him for all things—even for my illness and my blindness. If you glorify God for everything, you will experience joy."

He believes that the more one suffers with trust and thanksgiving, the more one draws near to Christ. For him, suffering is a gift because it deepened his communion with God.

St. Paisios also endured great pain—including tumors, hernias, and intestinal cancer in his later years. Yet he never complained. He says:

> "If you are grateful and glorify God in your illness, then your illness becomes a spiritual exercise and a crown of victory."

He often reminded others to say "Glory to God for all things"—not just when life was easy, but especially when life was hard.

Elder Aimilianos says:

> "The memory, the recollection, of God's activity is what moves us to praise and glorify Him. If I fail to remember what God has done for me, if I forget Who God is for me, then I cease to glorify Him. Even if I go to church and sing His praises with my mouth, it won't make any difference. If I've forgotten Him, my heart will remain far from such praises, unaffected by them, for it is a dead heart, and He is not the God of the dead, but of the living (Mt 22:32). Consequently, the remembrance of God is an essential element of true doxology."

3. Who is merciful to all your transgressions, Who heals all your diseases,

"*Who is merciful*": In the Bible and the Church Fathers, mercy (Greek: ἔλεος / eleos) wasn't just God feeling bad for someone. It is God running toward the suffering with healing in His hands. His mercy isn't passive—it's a movement, a touch, an embrace, a lifting.

Imagine a person lying in the dust, wounded and unable to rise, and the help of the Good Samaritan (Luke 10:30–37). In this parable, Jesus tells us about the nature of mercy. Mercy is the strong hand of God reaching down, cleaning his wounds, carrying him to safety, and paying for his healing. Remember also the paralytic when Jesus said, "Your sins are forgiven, take up your pallet and walk" (Matt 9: 2–6). Also, the sinful woman who entered where He was dining to anoint His feet (Luke 7:47–48) or Zacharias the tax collector (Luke 19:1–10). These are examples of how the early Christians understood God's mercy—not as leniency, but as an intervention, restoration, divine tenderness made visible.

St. Isaac the Syrian famously said:

> "Mercy is the name of God... The one who has mercy in his heart is the dwelling place of the Holy Spirit." (Ascetical Homilies, Homily 51)

So, for God to be *"merciful to all your transgressions"* means that He does not treat your sinfulness with justice alone, but with compassion and participates in your healing. He does not turn away from your sin, but moves toward you to restore and embrace you. You cannot be passive in receiving His mercy; you must be open to receive it.

St. John of Damascus writes:

> "God is not merciful because He is moved by us, as though He were changed. He is always good... always willing to save. Mercy is His natural, unchanging will." (*Exact Exposition of the Orthodox Faith*, Book I, ch. 14)

That means when God forgives our sins, He is not being lenient, but true to Himself—to His own love.

God is also the one *"Who heals all your diseases."* Mercy in the Orthodox tradition is restorative, not a legal pardon—it is a healing action. Sin is seen as a wound, and mercy is the treatment. So pray like David, who most likely is seeking a healing of his sinfulness, not necessarily a physical illness, but to be relieved of the passions that he has in himself.

St. Gregory of Nyssa teaches:

> "Sin is the disease of the soul; mercy is the hand of the divine Physician, who comes not to punish the sick, but to make them whole." (*Homilies on the Beatitudes*)

When God shows mercy, He is actively healing you, not simply overlooking your faults.

Beware, your pride may block it.

4. Who redeems your life from corruption, Who crowns you with mercy and compassion,

In the Orthodox tradition, the phrase *"redeems your life"* is deeply tied to the understanding of salvation, resurrection, and healing. It is not just poetic—it's a powerful statement of what God does for the whole person, soul and body.

The word *"redeems"* (Greek λυτροῦται) means to buy back, rescue, or deliver—especially someone enslaved or condemned. In Orthodox theology, your soul becomes enslaved by passions that lead you to sin—it needs to be rescued and liberated. Redemption is not legalistic as though God were exacting payment. Instead, it's an ongoing process of your soul's journey through repentance moving toward deification (theosis)—becoming partakers of the divine nature (2 Peter 1:4). It is God's love reaching down to lift you up, so that you may live forever in union with the Holy Trinity.

Through the Incarnation, by assuming human flesh, God entered fully into our suffering—and through the Cross and Resurrection, He opened the path for us to rise from corruption into life. This redemption is not merely from guilt, but from the very power of sin, death, and the devil. Christ's Incarnation, death, and Resurrection are the once-for-all, decisive acts by which He has redeemed you and all of humanity, defeated death, and set us free.

> "He gave Himself as a ransom for all…" (1 Timothy 2:6)

> "He has delivered us from the power of darkness…" (Colossians 1:13)

This is your foundation—the victory has already been won in Jesus Christ. Yet redemption is not only an event in the past; it also opens a pathway for your lifelong transformation, a journey that unfolds through your cooperation with God's grace. You are called to respond with repentance, to participate in the sacraments, to cultivate virtue, and to seek ever-deeper communion with Him. As St. Gregory of Nyssa writes,

> "We are always in the process of becoming—and redemption is the soul's journey back into the likeness of God."

The Greek word used in the phrase, *"from corruption,"* is φθορᾶς (phthoras)—which can mean decay, ruin, or death. St. Athanasius writes in *On the Incarnation*, referring to the Fall of mankind, that when Adam and Eve turned away from God,

> "Man, who was created in the image of the Word, was wasting away, and death had gained mastery over him... The Creator saw His creature falling into ruin, and in His love, He came to restore him."

Corruption, then, is the fallen state we inherit, of being bound to death (physically and spiritually) and enslaved to a tendency to sin, struggling to fulfill our true purpose, which is union with God. So when David says *"You redeem my life from corruption,"* he's not just thanking God for sparing him from danger—he's prophesying the ultimate victory over death and sin that Christ would accomplish.

The phrase, "*Who crowns you with mercy and compassion*," expresses the very heart of Orthodox spirituality: God not only forgives you when you repent—He lifts you up and clothes you with His own glory, a glory made of love.

To be crowned in Scripture often means to be exalted, honored, or set apart—like a king, a victor, or a beloved heir. But the crown David speaks of here is not made of gold or jewels. It is made of mercy (ἔλεος) and compassion (οἰκτιρμοί)—the two qualities that best describe God's heart toward His children.

The act of crowning has ancient Jewish roots: drawing from deep Jewish liturgical and covenantal traditions where crowns symbolized joy, devotion, and belonging to God—especially during the great feasts. The Jewish feast of Shavuot (Pentecost) is traditionally understood as the celebration of God's covenant with Israel at Mount Sinai. In the Midrash, this moment is described as a kind of wedding between God and His people. When the Israelites responded to God's Law by declaring, "We will do and we will hear" (Exodus 24:7), each person, according to Shabbat 88a in the Babylonian Talmud, was said to have received two crowns—one for obedience, and one for faith. These crowns symbolized joyful obedience, being set apart, covenantal love, and worship offered in devotion. This tradition beautifully parallels the Orthodox Christian understanding of your soul being crowned with mercy when it responds to God's Word in both hearing and doing—not as a reward for perfection, but as a gift of divine favor and grace.

Similarly, in Jewish wedding ceremonies, garlands or symbolic crowns were worn by both bride and groom, expressing joy, dignity, and blessing. This is reflected in Isaiah 61:10: "As a bridegroom decks himself with a garland, and as a bride adorns herself with her jewels…" In the Orthodox Church, this tradition is carried forward in the wedding service, where the couple is crowned with the στέφανα—symbols of a sacrificial love, the martyrdom of the will, and the royal dignity of union with Christ. In both traditions, to be crowned is to be joined in joyful covenant, offering one's life in love and faithfulness, as a living sacrifice of praise.

In Scripture, your praise becomes a kind of crown. It is an offering you make that not only enthrones God—as Psalm 22:3 says, "You are holy, enthroned on the praises of Israel"—but also lifts you up. Psalm 50:14 calls you to "Offer to God a sacrifice of praise," showing that true worship is not only external but deeply spiritual, often requiring the heart to bless God even in hardship. During Jewish festival worship, especially at the Feast of Sukkot (Leviticus 23:40), the people would rejoice before the Lord with garlands and palm branches, adorned with the beauty of creation as they gave thanks. This festive joy was more than celebration—it was a liturgical coronation, a sacred act in which God's mercy and covenant love were honored, and His people, in turn, were lifted into glory through their worship.

In your participation in Orthodox divine liturgy, this mystery continues with even greater depth. Your soul, even in sorrow or struggle, offers praise as a holy sacrifice. And God responds—not with mere approval, but by clothing your soul in mercy and compassion, just as the Psalm says. Your worship becomes a kind of divine exchange: your praise offered with faith, and His grace poured out in return. In this way, praise crowns both God and your soul with love, beauty, and communion.

5. Who satisfies your desire with good things; And your youth is renewed like the eagle's.

"*Who satisfies your desire with good things*" speaks of a God who fulfills not your shallow cravings, but the deepest hunger of your soul. The word for "desire" here, ἐπιθυμία (epithymia), refers to longing, appetite—the inner yearning at the core of every human being. In your fallen state, your desire is often misdirected, aimed at pleasure, pride, or possessions. But in Orthodox anthropology, desire is not evil; it was created by God to draw the soul toward Him. St. Gregory of Nyssa writes,

> "Desire is not evil in itself, but when guided by virtue,
> it becomes a chariot that carries the soul to God."

When purified and rightly ordered, your desire becomes the very path by which the soul ascends into communion with the divine.

Elder Aimilianos makes a beautiful point about the phrasing of this verse. It does not say "God satisfies your desires"—plural—but "your desire," singular. This speaks to a deeper transformation: after God raises up the soul, He changes it into one of single-minded longing, focused entirely on Him. As Aimilianos writes, when we become such a person—whose only desire is God—then God pours out all the truly good things: the peace of heart, the sweetness of His presence, the joy of the Holy Spirit, and the promise of the Kingdom.

As Christ says,

> "Seek first the Kingdom of God, and all these things
> will be added to you." (Luke 12:31)

The *"good things"* (ἀγαθά) of this verse are not material abundance or fleeting pleasures. They are the spiritual gifts God gives to you when you seek Him: the grace that heals, the light that illumines, the joy that does not fade. St. Augustine echoes this beautifully:

> "He fills your desire with good things—not with the
> vanities of earth, but with the blessings of heaven...
> the good that truly satisfies."

Only God can truly fill your soul, because only He is what your soul was made for. St. Maximus the Confessor teaches,

> "The soul is satisfied only when its longing is fixed
> upon the eternal and incorruptible—that is, on God
> Himself."

In this sense, satisfaction is not indulgence, but your soul being filled with what it was created for: to see the face of God and live.

The second half of the verse says, *"Your youth is renewed like the eagle's."* When you hear this, you are invited into an ancient image that spoke powerfully to people in biblical times. The renewal *"like the eagle"* carries deep meaning, and you are meant to see yourself in it.

First, think of the eagle's lifespan. Eagles live exceptionally long lives—often 20 to 30 years in the wild. To ancient eyes, they seemed almost immortal compared to other birds. You are being reminded that through God's grace, your life, too, is destined for something beyond decay and death.

Second, consider how the eagle molts. It sheds its old feathers and grows new ones, a process that would have looked like a miraculous renewal to those who watched it happen. You also are called to shed the old layers of your soul—your sins, your wounds, your weariness—and let God clothe you anew.

Third, after the eagle molts, it soars with renewed strength. So you, when you turn to God, are not only healed—you are strengthened, lifted up, and made ready to soar again with energy and courage you thought you had lost.

This is not just poetic encouragement for you. It is a promise. Just as the eagle's renewal is ongoing—happening again and again throughout its life—so God's renewal in you is not a one-time event. It is continuous, cyclical, woven into your spiritual life as you fall, rise, repent, and are healed again and again.

The eagle also became for the early Church a symbol of repentance and spiritual rebirth. You are meant to see yourself in this soaring creature: as you repent, you are shedding the old self, being washed and transformed by grace, and shining once again with the radiance you were created for.

And there's more. In ancient belief, the eagle could gaze directly at the sun without being blinded. You, too, are called to fix your eyes on the divine Light, to look upon the truth of God without fear or turning away. That's why St. John the Theologian is called the "Eagle of Patmos"—because his Gospel soars into the depths of the divine mystery. You are meant to follow.

St. Gregory the Theologian says of you:

> "The eagle is the image of the soul lifted up by grace,
> rising above the earth, looking toward eternity."

And St. Gregory of Nyssa tells you:

> "The eagle, when it becomes old, grows its feathers
> anew by bathing and turning its gaze to the sun—so
> too the soul, when it fixes its eye on the Divine Light,
> is renewed."

You are living the fulfillment of Isaiah's words:

> "But those who hope in the LORD will renew their
> strength. They will soar on wings like eagles; they
> will run and not grow weary, they will walk and not
> be faint." (Isaiah 40:31)

In Orthodox teaching, the eagle is a sign for you of resurrection—of your soul and your body being lifted up, freed from the earthbound passions, drawn toward heaven.

St. Augustine describes you when he says:

> "The eagle is the spiritual man who, after being
> weakened by sin, is made new by grace and lifted up
> again to the heights."

When David sings this Psalm, he is speaking about you. God does not just heal your wounds; He restores your strength. He rekindles your joy. He renews your very being. And this renewal begins for you even now, growing ever brighter until it reaches its fullness in the resurrection and the life of the age to come.

6. The Lord shows mercies
And judgment to all who are wronged.

"The Lord shows mercies" reveals the very heart of God's relationship with humanity. As Elder Aimilianos beautifully expresses:

"Deeds of mercy are the result of God's love, the fruits of His love in action… God is love, and so love is something that flows forth directly from His being."

God's mercy is not theoretical. It moves. It heals you, forgives you, intervenes for you, and transforms you. Mercy is not simply a legal pardon—it is the healing of your soul, and often even of your body. He liberates and defends those who are wronged. God lifts up the lowly and brings justice—not through human vengeance, but by restoring righteousness.

On the Cross, God did not merely pardon you from afar—He entered your suffering, bore your death, and gave you His life. As Elder Aimilianos writes:

"It is through His descent that we ascend… It is through His death that we live; through His suffering we are freed from suffering… These are truths that only become intelligible through experience; only to the extent that we have died and been resurrected by God's deeds of mercy, by His love."

In Orthodox theology, mercy and judgment are not opposites— they belong together. God's judgment is not punishment for its own sake; it is the setting right of what is broken. His judgment is always mingled with mercy. It seeks to heal, restore, and call both the oppressed and the oppressor back to life. As St. John of Damascus affirms:

"The judgment of God is just, but always mingled with mercy—for He desires not the death of the sinner, but that he should turn and live." (*Exact Exposition*, Book II, ch. 29)

The phrase *"to all who are wronged"* embraces more than those who are socially or politically oppressed. It speaks to the poor, the slandered, the betrayed, the persecuted—but also to those who are spiritually afflicted: crushed by grief, burdened by sin, bound by temptation, or tormented by demonic influence. God does not turn away from their pain. He moves toward it. He actively intervenes to vindicate, to comfort, and to restore. As St. Cyril of Alexandria declares:

> "God does not merely observe the wronged—He vindicates them. But He seeks also to save the wrong-doer, if he will turn."

Even when the oppression is internal—when the enemy is not another person, but sin, fear, sorrow, or despairGod's mercy remains near. St. Isaac the Syrian reminds you:

> "The Lord is near to every soul that suffers, even if
> it has fallen through its own fault. He does not turn
> away from sorrow."
> (*Ascetical Homilies*, Homily 46)

All of this reminds you that God's mercy is not weak—it is mighty. It is not passive—it is the active force by which He restores the world. In His mercy, He is both Judge and Healer, Father and Deliverer. And when you cry out, "Lord, have mercy," you are placing yourself entirely in the care of the One whose very nature is love in action.

7. He made known His ways to Moses,
The things He willed to the sons of Israel.

When you hear, *"He made known His ways to Moses,"* you are being invited to see how personally and profoundly God revealed Himself—not just through laws and commands, but through His very character, His presence, and His divine friendship. At the heart of this revelation stands the moment in Exodus 33–34, where Moses dares to ask God to show him His glory. In response, God does not give a visible form to behold. Instead, He reveals His Name—a verbal unveiling of His very essence:

> "The Lord, the Lord, compassionate and gracious,
> slow to anger, and abounding in mercy…"
> (Exodus 34:6)

This description, echoed directly in Psalm 102:8, teaches you that God's "ways" are not mere external rules. They are the outpouring of His mercy, patience, and love—the defining characteristics of how He relates to you and to all His people.

God also made His ways known to you through Moses by giving the Law at Mount Sinai. The Law was never meant to be a list of distant regulations; it was a path set before you, a guide for your journey toward holiness, justice, and worship. As St. Gregory of Nyssa writes:

> "In the giving of the Law, God revealed His ways—
> not merely as rules, but as a path leading the soul to
> life."

When you embrace this path, you are learning to live in harmony with God and with one another—to embody His love in every part of your life.

Yet even more intimately, God revealed His ways to Moses through friendship. Scripture tells you:

> "The Lord used to speak to Moses face to face, as a
> man speaks to his friend." (Exodus 33:11.

This shows you that to know God's ways is not only to follow commands or witness miracles—it is to enter into communion with Him. It is to experience a deep sharing between your heart and God's heart, your mind and His mind. If you seek Him as Moses did, you, too, are invited into this living friendship where God makes Himself known not from afar, but in love.

The second phrase, *"the things He willed to the sons of Israel,"* points you to the many ways God has acted on behalf of His people and revealed His desires for their life. In Greek, τὰ θελήματα αὐτοῦ means "His wills"—the actions He chose to take and the commands He gave for your good. These included the Torah, the Ten Commandments, and the liturgical instructions for sacrifices, festivals, and ritual purity—all meant to shape you, along with all Israel, into a holy nation living in covenant with God. They also included the moral and social justice laws that taught you to care for the poor, the widow, the orphan, and the stranger in your midst.

But God did not reveal His will only through commandments. He made it known through mighty acts in history—His *"willed actions"*—such as delivering His people from Egypt, parting the Red Sea, providing manna and water in the wilderness, and granting entry into the Promised Land. In these miracles, you see not only His power but His faithfulness, His providence, and His enduring love.

Through these "ways" and "willed actions," God was forming a relationship with His people—and with you—a relationship rooted in trust and obedience. This relationship would find its ultimate fulfillment and transformation in Christ, where you are invited not just to follow God's will, but to be united with it in love.

8. The Lord is compassionate and merciful, Slow to anger, and abounding in mercy.

When you hear these words, you're not just being taught a doctrine—you're being reminded of who God truly is. This verse isn't theory. These are the very words God spoke to Moses on Mount Sinai, when He revealed His name, His heart, His nature. And they echo through the psalms, through every liturgy, through every moment of your life.

He is "*compassionate*"—this means He sees your pain and draws near to it. The word speaks of a deep, inner sympathy, a God who does not stand far off, but enters your suffering with you.

He is "*merciful*"—not passively kind, but actively loving. His mercy is healing, restoring, and embracing. When you fall, when you are ashamed, when you feel ruined—His mercy meets you there.

He is "*slow to anger.*" You may be quick to assume God is angry with you—but He is not quick to condemn. He is patient with you, not willing that you perish, always giving time for your heart to turn back.

And He is "*abounding in mercy*"—πολυέλεος—not a little mercy, but overflowing kindness, far more than you deserve, far more than you even know how to ask for.

St. Gregory the Theologian reminds you:

> "God's mercy is greater than our sins—measureless, endless, unsearchable."

This verse is something you are meant to pray, to sing, to remember in your bones. The Orthodox Church repeats this verse in its hymns and services again and again, because you must learn to come before God not with terror, but with trust. His mercy is not earned—it is given. His arms are always open.

This psalm comes from David's own life—his failures, his regrets, his humiliations. Think of his worst moment: his sin with Bathsheba, and the death of her husband Uriah. And when Nathan the prophet confronted him, David didn't defend himself. He broke. He said, "I have sinned against the Lord," and Nathan answered, "The Lord has put away your sin." Just like that. Not without consequences—but with forgiveness that pierced the heart and stayed with him forever. That's why David could later cry out in Psalm 50: "Have mercy on me, O God, according to Your great mercy." He wasn't inventing poetry—he was writing from the place of deep personal redemption. And when God gave David a choice of punishments, David threw himself on God's mercy, saying, "Let me fall into the hand of the Lord, for His mercies are very great." (1 Chr. 21:13) He knew the character of the One he was trusting. He knew that even in discipline, God was more ready to forgive than to destroy.

You too must come to know this. When you have fallen, are suffering, feel abandoned, and struggle spiritually—remember David. He was betrayed by his own son. He lived in exile. He mourned deeply. He sinned grievously. But over and over again, he turned back. And every time, mercy was waiting.

When you read Psalm 102 and say, *"He is compassionate and merciful, Slow to anger, and abounding in mercy,"* don't read it as exaggeration. This is testimony. This is a man telling you that he was ruined—and God raised him up.

Elder Aimilianos reflects that when David uses these four attributes—compassionate, merciful, slow to anger, and rich in mercy—he is giving voice to the experience of his whole life. And you are invited to reflect on yours. Hasn't God been patient with you? Hasn't He shown you compassion when you deserved judgment? Haven't you seen His mercy meet you even when you felt furthest away?

This verse is calling you to remember. To trust. To return. To rest in the knowledge that your God is not waiting to punish you—but to heal you. Come to Him. He is already reaching for you.

9. He will not become angry to the end, Nor will He be wrathful forever;

"He will not become angry to the end." When you hear this, you're being reminded that God does not hold grudges—it is not who He is in His essence. Yes, you may experience His correction, His discipline, even what feels like His wrath—but know this: He does not get angry as we think of it. His purpose is never to condemn you, but always to heal you.

St. John of Damascus writes:

> "God is not angry by nature. He is said to be angry in a human way — to teach us that sin brings consequences. But His wrath is the work of love, not revenge." (*Exact Exposition of the Orthodox Faith*, Book 1, ch. 1)

So when you feel the weight of your own sin, when you feel the sting of correction, remember: it is not because God hates you—it is because He loves you too much to leave you in your brokenness. His anger is like a momentary flame, but His mercy is the eternal fire that restores and sanctifies.

"Nor will He be wrathful forever": This second phrase is telling you again, more gently: God is not like you. His wrath is not human rage. He does not lash out in fury. His wrath is His holiness reacting to sin—not to destroy you, but to awaken you, to bring you back. When we live in sin there are consequences. You may feel the weight of guilt or fear of punishment, but the purpose is not to drive you away. It is to call you home.

St. Isaac the Syrian says:

> "Do not call God just... His justice is not as ours. His mercy is His justice. The punishment of sin is the scourge of love—to awaken the soul." (*Ascetical Homilies*, Homily 90)

Think about that. What you sometimes experience as punishment may actually be love in disguise—God's relentless mercy, shaking your soul awake.

This is what the Church teaches you about repentance and salvation. There is nothing you've done that God cannot forgive—unless you refuse to turn back to Him. If you ignore His presence, if you harden your heart and reject His love, only then do you place yourself outside His mercy. Not because He has stopped loving you, but because you've closed the door.

Orthodoxy does not teach that hell is a place where God stops loving you. Hell is what the soul feels when it has rejected love—when it refuses communion, yet cannot escape God's presence. His love continues, even in that pain. He desires not the death of the sinner, but that you turn and live.

That's why in the Church you keep crying out, "Lord, have mercy." Not because God is harsh. Not because He is unwilling to forgive. But because His mercy is greater than anything you could ever bring before Him. Because His mercy triumphs over judgment (James 2:13).

So come before Him—not in terror, but in trust. His anger is fleeting. His mercy endures forever.

**10. He did not deal with us according to our sins,
Nor reward us according to our transgressions;**

**11. For according to the height of heaven from earth,
So the Lord reigns in mercy over those who fear Him;**

**12. As far as the east is from the west,
So He removes our transgressions from us.**

These verses are meant to bring you deep comfort and stir up a profound joy within your soul. They remind you just how vast God's mercy truly is. Whatever has happened in your life—whether through trial or failure—nothing has been outside of God's loving providence. Even your sins, however many or grievous, are not stronger than His mercy. Everything that unfolds in your life, He allows for your salvation. And that should awaken joy, not shame.

The psalm declares, *"He did not deal with us according to our sins, nor reward us according to our transgressions."* When you reflect on this, you are hearing the very truth that every repentant heart clings to: God does not treat you as your sins deserve. He doesn't repay evil for evil. He doesn't hold your past over your head. His justice is not the world's justice—it is not retribution, but restoration. His desire is not to get even, but to make you whole.

This means His mercy is not a transaction. He is not keeping score. He does not offer forgiveness as a reward for good behavior. He gives you what you do not deserve: love, healing, and a new beginning. Think of the father in the parable of the Prodigal Son. He didn't wait for an apology to embrace his son. He ran to him, embraced him mid-confession, and clothed him in dignity again. That's your God.

As St. Isaac the Syrian writes:

> "The one who knows his own sin and God's mercy knows that even if he lived a hundred lives, he could not repay God for one hour of forgiveness."

If you've tasted that mercy, then you know this truth. You know that His forgiveness is more than pardon—it's resurrection.

So when David says, *"according to the height of heaven from earth,"* he is telling you that God's mercy is beyond your reach to measure. You could spend a lifetime climbing, and never find the top. That's how far His compassion stretches over you when you humble yourself before Him.

The phrase *"He reigns in mercy"* uses the word ἐκραταίωσε— meaning He has made mercy strong and established it. His rule is not harsh or cold; it is mercy itself. Mercy is not God's weakness—it is His power. As St. Isaac the Syrian so beautifully puts it: "Mercy is the throne of God."

And who receives this mercy? Those who fear Him. But you must understand— this fear is not terror. It is reverent love. It is the awe that floods your soul when you begin to realize how holy God is—and how merciful He still is toward you. It is the trembling that comes not from dread, but from wonder.

As St. Symeon the New Theologian says:

> "To fear God is to tremble at His love—to stand in
> awe of His mercy, not to run from it."

And now comes one of the most healing promises in all of Scripture: "*As far as the east is from the west, so He removes our transgressions from us.*" Think about that. East and West never meet. You can travel east forever and never reach the west. That is how far God has cast your sins from you—immeasurably far, eternally distant, completely gone.

And the verb is active: He removed them. You didn't do it. He did. You don't save yourself. You don't cleanse yourself. He is the Lamb of God who takes away the sin of the world—including yours.

In Orthodox theology, forgiveness doesn't mean God just forgets your sin or covers it over. It means He actually heals you. He restores your soul so deeply that you are made new.

As St. Gregory of Nyssa said:

> "He makes the soul new, as if it had never sinned—
> not by covering it over, but by truly restoring it."
> (*On the Beatitudes*, Homily 5)

You are not your past. You are not your shame. You are His beloved child, cleansed and crowned with mercy.

So what should your response be? Not guilt. Not hesitation. But humble gratitude and wholehearted repentance. These verses are not abstract theology—they are an invitation. Do not let fear keep you at a distance. Do not believe the lie that your sins define you. If He has cast them "*as far as the east is from the west,*" then you are free. You are forgiven.

But that freedom isn't permission to remain in sin—it is strength to rise from it. So don't hesitate to run to Him like the prodigal son. Let His mercy raise you up. And live each day with joy, with reverence, and with thanksgiving—because your God reigns in mercy, and you are forever held in the power of His love.

13. As a father has compassion on his children,
So the Lord has compassion on those who fear Him,

When you hear this verse, you're being invited to remember what the love of a true father feels like—or what it should feel like: watchful, tender, strong, and constant. In the ancient world, a father's compassion was seen as one of the most instinctive, fierce, and enduring forms of love. David uses this image to tell you something astonishing: this is how God loves you. His love isn't distant or abstract. It's not cold or conditional. It is fatherly—intimate, warm, protective, and unfailing.

He has compassion on you—not just once in the past, not just when you are doing well, but always. The verb used here (οἰκτείρει) is active and ongoing. It means He is continually moved by love for you. Like a father who watches his child stumble and runs to help—not with scolding, but with tears of concern—so your heavenly Father draws near to you in your weakness. His compassion is not merely an emotion—it's a movement toward you, even when you've fallen.

Especially when you've fallen.

And to whom does He show this kind of love? To those who fear Him. But remember: this fear is not dread. It's reverence. It's the awe that grips you when you realize how holy and merciful God truly is. It's humility—the quiet awareness of how little you deserve, and how freely He gives. It's trust—the trust of a child who knows his father will always love him, even when he messes up.

St. Symeon the New Theologian says:

> "To fear God is to fear wounding the love of the Father who gave us everything."

That's the kind of fear that draws you closer to Him—not the kind that drives you away.

Elder Aimilianos also reflects on this verse, saying that among all human relationships, the bond between parent and child is the strongest. You know what it's like to love a child—to make sacrifices, to worry, to hope, to weep. Now realize that God loves you with even greater intensity. The psalmist chose this image—the clearest and strongest comparison possible—to help you begin to grasp how God sees you: not as a servant to be punished, but as a beloved child to be healed, restored, and held.

And now, you must ask yourself: Do you love God the way a child loves a parent? Do you long to please Him—not out of fear, but out of love? Do you trust Him the way a child trusts a father's embrace?

Christ pushes this even further when He says,

> "He who loves son or daughter more than Me is not worthy of Me." (Matthew 10:37)

It's not that you shouldn't love your children deeply—you should. But now He is asking you: Do you love Me as deeply as that? Do you trust Me, cling to Me, honor Me with that same devotion?

Because He already loves you more than you can imagine—more than you love your own children. He is the Father who runs to you, embraces you, clothes you with dignity, and calls you home.

Let that truth break your fear and awaken your heart.

When you pray these words, you're being reminded of something profoundly comforting: God knows you completely. He knows your makeup, your frailty, your limits—not as a distant observer, but as your Creator. He remembers the day He formed you. He doesn't forget what you are.

The language of this verse echoes Genesis 2:7:

> "Then the Lord God formed man from the dust of
> the ground, and breathed into his nostrils the breath
> of life."

Unlike the rest of creation, which came into being through a word, you were formed. God stooped low, metaphorically speaking, and shaped you with His own hands—gently, intentionally, lovingly. He breathed His own life into you. That breath still lives in you.

St. Irenaeus of Lyons says the hands of God are the Son and the Spirit. When God formed you from the dust, He did so through Christ and the Holy Spirit. You are not a mistake. You are not an afterthought. You were shaped for communion—created to reflect divine beauty, reason, freedom, and longing for the good.

So when Scripture says, "He knows how He formed you," it means He understands you down to the depths. He knows your capacity for greatness— and your capacity for failure. He remembers that you are both made of earth and filled with breath from heaven. He does not expect perfection from you. He expects dependence, humility, and trust.

Even more: God knew you would fall. He knew your weakness before He ever gave you life—and He still made you. And not only did He form you, but He prepared the way back when you would stray. Christ's coming was not Plan B. It was always part of the plan of love. That's how deep His mercy goes.

"He remembers you are dust." These are not words of rejection. They are words of compassion. They remind you that you are not invincible. You are not a god. You are a created being— finite, fragile, in constant need of God. But that doesn't lessen your value. In fact, it magnifies His mercy.

St. Basil the Great says:

> "God shows compassion not because we deserve it,
> but because He made us and sustains us."

You don't need to earn His kindness. You need only remember that you are dust—and turn to Him in sincerity. His mercy doesn't come because of your greatness. It flows because of Him.

You will return to dust someday. Your body will fail. But even then, you are not abandoned. The God who formed you from the earth is the One who will raise you up from it. He remembers what you are—and He still chooses to love you, to forgive you, and to restore you.

Elder Aimilianos once said:

> "He will look upon you in the light of what you are
> made. He knows that, being a vessel of clay, you are
> fragile—like a pitcher that breaks at the fountain and
> quickly returns to the dust." (cf. Ecclesiastes 12:1)

And so, when you fall, do not despair. When you are weak, do not pretend to be strong. Come to Him as you are. Dust, yes—but dust He shaped in love, and dust He will glorify in Christ.

**15. As for man, his days are like grass,
As a flower of the field, so he flourishes;**

16. For the wind passes through it, and it shall not remain; And it shall no longer know its place.

17. But the mercy of the Lord is from age to age upon those who fear Him, And His righteousness upon children's children.

These verses invite you to face your own mortality—not in fear, but with reverence and hope. You flourish like a flower in the field—briefly radiant, impossibly delicate, breathtaking in your beauty—and yet so easily scattered by the wind. Like a cherry blossom in spring, your life may shine gloriously for a moment, and then vanish without a trace.

"As a flower of the field, so he flourishes": You may recall times when you stood in the spring beneath cherry trees in full bloom. In Japan there is a national celebration at that special time of the year—their beauty seems to stop their world for a moment. Strangers, co-workers, and families gather in joy just to behold the petals, their beauty that seems to last only for a moment.

As with all flowering trees, observe how quickly those beautiful blossoms fall. The wind scatters them. You return days later, and the tree has forgotten it ever bloomed. *"The wind passes through it, and it shall not remain."*

So it is with your life. You rise, you flourish, you grow. Then age comes, your form changes, the face fades, and eventually, you return to the earth. Even your place—the people, the places, the rhythm of life—goes on without you. You are no longer remembered in the same way. "*It shall no longer know its place.*"

Because even as your days pass like grass, "*the mercy of the Lord is from age to age upon those who fear Him.*" His mercy is not fragile. His love does not fade. While you are like the cherry blossom—brief and beautiful—He is the root, the ground, the spring that brings you back to life. He remembers you, even when the world forgets. His love is not brief—it is eternal.

The fear of the Lord here is not dread—it is reverent love. It is awe that you, a creature of dust, are held in the mercy of the eternal God. His mercy is not just for today—it stretches across generations. As the cherry blossoms return each year in their season, so does God's faithfulness return again and again to your family, your children, and your children's children. He does not forget them. He does not abandon you. His righteousness, His justice, His goodness—it reaches far beyond your life.

You are reminded too that this mercy is not just poetic—it is powerful. The mercy of God renews you. Like the cherry tree that looks dead through the winter, your soul may grow cold, weary, or numb—but His grace can bloom again, sometimes suddenly, filling your life with beauty you thought you had lost. Your youth is renewed like the eagle's (Psalm 102:5), and grace overtakes grief.

And there is even more. Because you know the full truth that the psalmist only glimpsed: the mystery of resurrection. You will rise again. Your body may fall like a blossom on the breeze, but it will not remain in the dust. Christ has promised it. The tree that looked dead will bloom again. What is sown in corruption will be raised in incorruption… what is sown in weakness will be raised in power (1 Corinthians 15:42–43).

Elder Aimilianos once wrote:

> "Though your life on earth is tragic, you will live. God's hands shall lovingly take up the dust of the earth, and the fleeting and the finite will be wedded to the eternal and the infinite."

That is your hope. That is your future. Your fragility is not your end—it is the gateway to glory.

So remember this when you see the cherry blossom, or when the wind moves through the branches of your life. Let that moment awaken your soul—not to sorrow, but to joy. Because your life is not brief—it is eternal. Because the beauty you now taste is only a shadow of the glory that will come.

And because your God remembers you.

18. To such as keep His covenant
And remember His commandments, to do them.

If you remember what He has taught and walk in His commandments, God's promise of renewal—whether through repentance or beyond death—is extended to you. His love for you is unconditional, but His covenant is relational. To *keep His covenant* means that you live in faithful obedience—not out of fear or legalism, but as an act of love, expressed through trust and the choices you make each day.

"If you love Me, keep My commandments," Jesus said (John 14:15). These words are for you. Your love for God is not proven by sentiment alone, but by the life you live in response to His mercy. The promise that His righteousness will rest upon your children's children is not automatic—it is connected to your faithfulness. What you do now, how you live now, matters across generations.

In Scripture, to *"remember"* is never passive. It doesn't mean simply recalling a fact—it means letting that memory shape you. When the psalm says, *"remember His commandments to do them,"* it's calling you to live with purpose. You are not asked to remember and admire, but to remember and act.

St. Cyril of Jerusalem writes:

> "The soul that truly remembers God's commandments will live by them—and in so doing, abide in the mercy of the Lord" (*Catechetical Lectures*, Lecture 6).

To keep His covenant is to walk with Him—to trust Him, to return to Him when you fall, to let your entire life be marked by reverent love. This is the kind of life that opens your soul to receive His mercy, not just for today, but into eternity—and extending even into the lives of those who come after you.

You are not just living for yourself. Your faithfulness now becomes a seed of grace in future generations. God's righteousness flows across time, and your obedience becomes a vessel through which He blesses others. Let this awaken you—not in fear, but in joy. You are loved, and you are called to respond.

19. The Lord prepared His throne in heaven,
And His Kingdom rules over all.

"Lord prepared His throne in heaven" is asking you to lift your eyes from your own weakness and sorrow to the majesty of God enthroned above. After being reminded of His mercy, His patience, His forgiveness, and how gently He remembers that you are dust, you are now invited to look up—to see the glory of the One who rules all things.

His throne is not built by men, and it does not belong to this earth. It has been prepared by God Himself—firmly established in the heavens, in the place of unshakable justice, radiant peace, and perfect glory.

As the Lord declares in Isaiah:

> "Heaven is My throne, and earth is My footstool."
> (Isaiah 66:1).

No storm in this world can unsettle Him. No power of darkness can challenge His reign. His throne is secure.

What is so striking here is this: the very same God who forgives all your sins, who heals your diseases, who surrounds you with mercy is the One who sits enthroned above all creation. His power and His mercy are not opposites. They are perfectly united. The throne you gaze upon is not cold. It is not distant. It is the throne of a Father.

St. Isaac the Syrian writes:

> "Mercy is the scepter by which He rules."
> (*Ascetical Homilies*, Homily 74)

This is why you do not need to fear God's power. You can trust it. Because the One who governs all things also crowns you with love and compassion. You are held by the same hands that hold the universe.

"And His Kingdom rules over all": This reign is not limited to heaven. It extends to all things: to the earth, to the nations, to your life, to your thoughts, to your joys and fears. Everything is under His care—not just in theory, but in reality. Even when the world seems chaotic, even when your life feels uncertain, His dominion is real, steady, and present. You are not adrift. He rules over all.

In the fullness of time, this verse points to Christ the King— the Lord who ascended into heaven and took His seat at the right hand of the Father. He now reigns in glory, and nothing is outside His authority.

As Isaiah prophesied of Him: "Of the increase of His government and of peace there shall be no end." (Isaiah 9:7)

So when you feel weak, or forgotten, or surrounded by confusion, remember this: your life is under the care of a King whose throne is unshakable and whose rule is mercy. You are not just seen by God—you are governed by His goodness. Lift your eyes to His throne. Let your heart rest in the confidence that the One who reigns above is also the One who loves you most.

20. Bless the Lord, all you His angels,
   Mighty in strength, who do His word,
   So as to hear the voice of His words.

When you say *"Bless the Lord, all you His angels,"* let your heart be lifted toward the heavens—beholding the Lord's mercy, His patience, His justice, and His eternal throne. You are invited to gaze even higher. David, overwhelmed by God's greatness, turns his eyes to the angelic hosts and calls them to bless the Lord. Not because they've forgotten to do so, but because their praise is pure, constant, and radiant. In joining your voice to theirs, you're invited into the heavenly liturgy—a worship that never ceases.

You've heard their cry before. In Isaiah's vision, and in the Revelation given to St. John, they cry out: "Holy, holy, holy is the Lord of Hosts; heaven and earth are full of His glory" (Isaiah 6:3; Revelation 4:8). When you, like David, call on the angels to bless the Lord, you are not just making a poetic gesture—you are uniting heaven and earth in a single chorus. And you are meant to join them.

"Mighty in strength…": The angels are mighty—not just in power, but in purity, purpose, and unshakable obedience. Their strength is not self-contained. It flows from their unbroken union with God's will.

As St. Gregory the Theologian says,

> "The angels are mighty not in power alone, but in the purity of their service and the constancy of their praise." (Oration 38: On the Theophany)

That's where true strength lies—not in dominance, but in love, humility, and unwavering devotion.

If you want to know what strength looks like in God's Kingdom, look to the angels. They are not distracted. They are not half-hearted. Their power is their attention, their faithfulness, their joyful obedience.

"Who do His word… to hear the voice of His words": This phrase is striking in its clarity. Be like the angels who do and hear God's word. They are not passive.

They are ready—always listening, always attentive, always prepared to move the instant His voice stirs. They don't argue. They don't hesitate. They don't delay. Their obedience is not blind—it is loving and intelligent. They serve because they see the glory of the One they serve. And they do it with joy.

This is what your obedience is meant to resemble. You're not called to be a servant of fear, but a child who listens—whose ears are attuned to the voice of the Father, whose heart is soft, ready to move when love commands. The angels remind you that holiness is not just about stillness—it's about readiness.

Listening deeply. Moving swiftly. Loving truly.

So now, as you stand before the Lord in prayer, lift your voice alongside the angels. Call on them to bless the Lord—not because they need the reminder, but because you need to join their song. And as you bless the Lord, let your soul become like theirs: focused, strong, and wholly surrendered to His will.

21. Bless the Lord, all you His hosts, His ministers who do His will;

The psalm expands your vision even further. You are being invited to see not just the angels, but the full grandeur of God's creation—both seen and unseen—called into the chorus of praise.

The word *"hosts"* (Hebrew tzva'ot, Greek δυνάμεις) refers to the vast armies of heaven: angels, archangels, and every spiritual power that serves God. But it doesn't stop there. It includes the cosmic order—the stars that shine, the sun that rises, the moon that marks the seasons. All of it, all of them, glorify the One who made them.

"The heavens declare the glory of God" (Psalm 18:1 / 19:1). And you are part of that creation. You, too, are summoned to take your place in this grand procession of worship.

When you hear the word "leitourgoi," meaning "ministers," know that it doesn't refer only to heavenly beings. It also includes the prophets, the priests, the saints, and even you, if you are willing to serve the will of God in your life. The Church teaches that this liturgical service spans heaven and earth. The angels serve in the heavenly temple, the saints offer praise before the throne, and you are invited to offer your own life as liturgy—through worship, through obedience, through love.

St. Gregory of Nyssa says it beautifully:

> "To serve the will of God is the highest calling— whether in heaven or on earth. All who do so are united in one liturgy of praise." (*On the Lord's Prayer*, Homily 5)

That includes you. When you follow God's will, however small the act may seem—whether it is patient kindness, silent prayer, forgiveness, or courage—you are joining the eternal liturgy. You are blessing the Lord with your life.

You may not always feel this. Your daily routine may seem ordinary. But every time you offer yourself in humility and faithfulness, you become a minister of praise. You are united with the angels, the saints, and all creation, in a single song that rises to the throne of God.

So don't underestimate your role. Your obedience, your repentance, your love— these are not isolated efforts. They are your way of entering the great liturgy of heaven. Every time you choose what is good, every time you resist pride and respond with mercy, you are blessing the Lord.

Let this verse remind you: you are not alone in your worship. You are part of a heavenly host. Let your life become a liturgy—an offering of praise.

22. Bless the Lord, all His works, In all places of His dominion; Bless the Lord, O my soul.

This is the psalm's great doxology—its final and most sweeping call to worship. Now, you are invited to join not only the angels and the hosts of heaven, but all of creation in blessing the Lord. Every star, every tree, every wave, every breath of wind is being summoned to praise—and so are you.

When you hear "*all His works*," understand that it means everything He has made. That includes the heavens and the earth, the mountains and the seas, the animals and the angels—and your very own soul. Creation is not silent. The natural world is alive with praise. As Psalm 150 declares: "Let everything that has breath praise the Lord."

St. Basil the Great says:

> "All creation, through its beauty and order, silently sings of the Creator. When man joins in with understanding, the harmony becomes complete." (*Hexaemeron*, Homily 5)

So you are being invited to join the harmony. Your praise is not small. When you lift your voice in worship, you are completing the cosmic song. You are aligning your soul with the stars.

There is no part of the universe outside God's dominion. His reign is everywhere—across galaxies and oceans, through time and eternity, in the temple and the street, in the sanctuary and in your suffering. Even in the hidden, painful places of your life, He is still King, and His mercy still reigns.

That's why blessing the Lord is not confined to a church service or a special hour. You are called to carry this praise into every corner of your life. Wherever you are, whatever you're facing, you are in the place of His dominion. And in that place, you can bless Him.

And now, after calling angels, hosts, and all creation into the song, the psalm circles back—quietly, intimately—to you. David ends where he began: *"Bless the Lord, O my soul."* After seeing all that God is—His compassion, His mercy, His justice, His throne, His kingdom—how could you not respond? You have seen the majesty of His love. You have been reminded of who He is. And now, you must speak to your own soul and say: Bless Him. Bless Him with everything you are.

Because worship begins there—in the depths of your soul. And when your soul is moved, when your heart bows low in reverent love, the rest of your life will follow.

So bless Him. In sorrow and in joy. In weakness and in strength. In the stillness of prayer and in the chaos of your day. Let every breath be praise.

"Bless the Lord, O my soul."

Summary

Psalm 102 (103) is a hymn of amazing tenderness and transcendent power—and it begins with you. It begins in the secret place of your soul, where you are called to rise—from forgetfulness into remembrance, from sorrow into praise. From the very first words, *"Bless the Lord, O my soul,"* to the final echo of that same line, you are taken on a journey: from personal gratitude to cosmic worship, from your own frailty to the throne of God's eternal mercy.

When you are struggling—with pain, with loss, with regret or weakness—this psalm is for you. It is a lifeline when your strength fails. It was not written in comfort, but from the depths of human sorrow. David knew what you feel at times: sin, betrayal, illness, fear, grief. And yet, from that place he could say: *"He heals all your diseases... He redeems your life from corruption."* These are are the living testimony of a soul who was rescued again and again.

This psalm assures you that God does not treat you as you deserve. He lifts you up with steadfast love. Even when you feel as fleeting as a flower, as frail as dust, even when the world forgets you—God remembers. He remembers how He formed you. He remembers your pain, your limits, your need for mercy. And instead of judgment, He crowns you with compassion.

In your own moments of emptiness, dryness, or brokenness, this psalm calls you not to despair—but to bless the Lord. Even when you don't feel it. Even when your heart is tired. Blessing God is not about emotion—it is an act of trust, a movement of the soul, a whisper of love in the silence.

As St. Theophan the Recluse reminds you:

> "Offer God your faithfulness; feelings will come in
> time, if He wills."

But even more, this psalm tells you that your worship is not alone. When you bless the Lord, you are joining a mighty chorus. The angels are blessing Him. The saints are blessing Him. The stars, the wind, the trees, the seas—all His works in every place of His dominion are lifting up praise. You are not voiceless. You are not forgotten. You are part of the eternal liturgy of heaven.

So bless Him. From your soul, with all that is in you. In weakness and in strength. In joy and in sorrow. Let your voice rise, and join the everlasting song:

"Bless the Lord, O my soul."

PSALM 142 (143)

*1 A psalm by David, when his son persecuted him.**
O Lord, hear my prayer; Give ear to my supplication in Your
truth; Answer me in Your righteousness;

2 Do not enter into judgment with Your servant,
For no one living shall become righteous in Your sight.

3 For the enemy persecuted my soul;
He humbled my life to the ground;
He caused me to dwell in dark places as one long dead,

4 And my spirit was in anguish within me;
My heart was troubled within me.

5 I remembered the days of old,
And I meditated on all Your works;
I meditated on the works of Your hands.

6 I spread out my hands to You;
My soul thirsts for You like a waterless land.

(Pause)

7 Hear me speedily, O Lord;
My spirit faints within me;
Turn not Your face from me,
Lest I become like those who go down into the pit.

8 Cause me to hear Your mercy in the morning,
For I hope in You;
Make me know, O Lord, the way wherein I should walk,
For I lift up my soul to You.

9 Deliver me from my enemies, O Lord,
For to You I flee for refuge.

10 Teach me to do Your will, for You are my God;
Your good Spirit shall guide me in the land of uprightness.

11 For Your name's sake, O Lord, give me life;
In Your righteousness You shall bring my soul out of affliction.

12 In Your mercy You shall destroy my enemies;
You shall utterly destroy all who afflict my soul,
For I am Your servant.

Commentary

Psalm 142 (LXX) is attributed to David. It is traditionally thought to have been written by David during his time of fleeing from King Saul, but it could certainly also apply to the later distress caused by Absalom's rebellion, which was a deeply painful and traumatic time in David's life.

It captures the deep anguish of the soul when faced with trials, enemies, and spiritual desolation. The psalmist cries out to God for refuge and guidance, acknowledging his own helplessness while affirming God's righteousness and faithfulness.

The psalm is structured as a prayer for God's intervention, beginning with a plea for deliverance from enemies and moving toward an earnest confession of trust in God's goodness. As David expresses his solitude and feeling of abandonment, he simultaneously holds on to the hope that God's mercy will lead him to safety and restoration. Psalm 142 invites you to identify with the psalmist's experience, offering a model for seeking God's grace as you rise in the morning seeking help and guidance as you prepare for the activities of your worldly life.

1. A psalm by David, when his son persecuted him.
O Lord, hear my prayer;
Give ear to my supplication in Your truth;
Answer me in Your righteousness;

When you cry out, *"O Lord, Hear my prayer,"* you are inviting God into the depths of your life, acknowledging His presence, and seeking a deeper relationship with Him.

Prayer is not just a request—it is an act of communion with God, aligning your heart with His will and opening yourself to His transforming grace. By invoking God's faithfulness and righteousness, you entrust yourself to His unwavering love and justice, knowing that He will respond with mercy, wisdom, and holiness.

Prayer is not simply about asking for your desires to be fulfilled, but about aligning yourself with God's will—recognizing that His response may differ from your expectations. The focus is on God's faithfulness and righteousness, trusting that He will always respond in the way that is best for you, according to His wisdom and love.

Though God hears all prayers, the cry to "hear" is not about informing Him of something He doesn't already know. Rather, it is a plea for active communion with Him. You are inviting God to draw near, to engage with you, and to intervene in your life in a personal and transformative way.

Jesus assures us,

> "Ask, and it will be given to you; seek, and you will find; knock, and it will be opened to you." (Matthew 7:7)

God hears our prayers and promises He will respond, though His timing and manner may be beyond our immediate understanding.

Reciting this psalm, you are asking God to respond "*in Your Truth*." The Greek word ἀλήθεια (aletheia) used here is translated more typically as "truth." So David is asking God to guide him to the "*truth*" of God's faithfulness, the assurance of His promises, and His guidance.

In this context, David is highlighting not just God's faithfulness and righteousness but also His unchanging, eternal nature. He is asking God to respond based on His perfect, trustworthy character—the God who is always true to His promises, who will never abandon you or fail to fulfill His word.

Christ Himself is called "*the Truth*" in John 14:6—the fulfillment of God's eternal truth and faithfulness manifested in the Person of the Word made flesh. Thus, when you pray for God to answer "*in Your righteousness*," you are seeking divine intervention in accordance with God's perfect will, which is ultimately revealed in Christ.

When you pray "*Answer me in Your righteousness*," you are acknowledging that God's righteousness is the very foundation of His nature and actions. Don't mistake His righteousness as simply moral correctness or adherence to rules; it is the perfect expression of His love and divine goodness. It encompasses His justice, mercy, and holiness, and is intrinsically tied to His desire to restore, heal, and redeem creation. It is through His righteous love that salvation is made possible, as He offers not only justice but also the opportunity for His creatures to experience His unfailing grace and restorative love. God's righteousness, then, is the ultimate expression of His deep love for humanity, drawing all people into a relationship with Him, where His justice, mercy, and healing are perfectly intertwined.

St. Gregory the Theologian writes,

> "God's righteousness is not a mere legal judgment, but it is a righteousness that lifts us up to His holiness, making us partakers of His divine nature." (*Oration 41*, on the Holy Spirit)

St. Gregory points to theosis (deification), which is a central concept in Orthodox concept of salvation. Through God's righteousness, He invites us into union with Him, not merely as servants or subjects but as partakers in His divine nature (2 Peter 1:4). This means that, through Christ and the Holy Spirit, we are called to be transformed—to share in God's holiness and become partakers of the eternal, divine life. God's righteousness, therefore, is not just about maintaining moral order, but about uniting humanity with the divine and making us share in God's life and holiness.

Asking for an answer in God's righteousness, you recognize that God's righteousness is a perfect expression of His love and holiness. You are asking God to respond not just according to a set of rules, but according to His transformative grace, restoring goodness, and unfailing love, leading to the restoration of your relationship with Him.

As you recite this psalm in prayer, you are opening your heart to receive His grace, not only seeking His help for the new day but desiring that He will transform your heart and life. You are recognizing that a life lived in God according to what He wills requires His help.

Jesus says,

> "I am the vine, you are the branches. He who abides in Me, and I in him, bears much fruit; for apart from Me you can do nothing." (John 15:5)

As you seek His help each morning, remember that prayer is not only about changing your circumstances, but about allowing God to shape and transform you according to His divine plan.

2. Do not enter into judgment with Your servant, For no one living shall become righteous in Your sight.

"*Do not enter into judgment with Your servant,*" means you are asking God not to judge you according to your actions or merits, but seek His mercy instead. This plea reflects an awareness of your human weaknesses, imperfections, and sinful nature. You are asking God, with His great love and compassion, to look upon you with His mercy.

You are also asking God to look into your heart, to reveal your faith among your weaknesses, and to guide you toward repentance. You are also placing your hope in God's loving-kindness. His judgment, when it comes, is always tempered by His desire for your healing and salvation.

"For no one living shall become righteous in Your sight," is a recognition of the condition of all humanity. You are confessing that you know you are incapable of achieving perfect righteousness by your own strength. Even with your best efforts, you recognize that you fall short of God's holiness and justice.

You are agreeing with Paul when he says,

> "As it is written: 'None is righteous, no, not one.'"
> (Romans 3:10)

By recognizing that *"no one living shall become righteous,"* you are humbling yourself before God, acknowledging that salvation comes only through His mercy and not through personal achievement or self-righteousness.

3. For the enemy persecuted my soul;
   He humbled my life to the ground;
   He caused me to dwell in dark places
   as one long dead,

When you pray, *"The enemy has persecuted my soul, he has humbled my life to the ground,"* you are expressing a spiritual struggle you experience in the trials and tribulations of your daily life while seeking to become like Christ. You know you need God's help, but it may seem distant. You desire greater meaning in your daily activities. You feel that your mind is consumed with worldly cares, making it hard to focus on God. Your heart also is filled with desires that lead you away from being Christ-like, draining your energy, leaving you feeling stressed and restless. This expresses a feeling that something is relentlessly chasing you, preventing you from experiencing the joy and peace that God promises.

The "*enemy*" includes temptations, external hardships, and the spiritual struggles that seek to pull you away from God. You feel as though these forces are unending, chasing you down and weighing you down, making it hard to find peace or hope. The image of being "*humbled my life to the ground*" conveys a sense of helplessness, where you are unable to rise on your own.

This is a plea for God's intervention, not one of hopelessness. By honestly bringing your struggles before God, you are acknowledging that only He has the power to lift you from this condition and restore you. You want God to act with His strength and mercy to provide the support and deliverance you cannot find by your own efforts.

The phrase, "*He caused me to dwell in dark places as one long dead*," expresses a sense of spiritual confusion and a lack of clarity about the direction. It expresses a spiritual condition of feeling trapped in a dark room, unable to find the exit because the darkness surrounds you. God's light seems absent, and you are failing to recognize His presence, you find yourself uncertain of the meaning behind the events unfolding in your life. This *darkness* is the spiritual condition you are encountering when you feel distant from God, weighed down by your own thoughts, struggling to find a way forward or feel the warmth of His love.

The phrase "*as one long dead*" reflects a sense of hopelessness, buried under the burden of your life's situation and forgotten.

Thinking about heavenly things may seem impossible as your worldly concerns dominate your reality. Yet, in expressing this, you are crying out to God for help. By acknowledging the darkness and calling on God, you are placing your trust in His ability to bring you out of it. You know He is the light, that even in the deepest darkness He can guide you by the light of His grace and love towards eternal life with Him in His Kingdom.

Jesus says,

> "I am the light of the world. Whoever follows me will
> not walk in darkness, but will have the light of life."
> (John 8:12)

4. And my spirit was in anguish within me; My heart was troubled within me.

"My spirit was in anguish within me," expresses a sense of being overwhelmed, feeling spiritually drained and distant from God. The weight of all your life's challenges, disappointments, and sins can leave you spiritually and emotionally troubled. These may cause you to feel as though there is little hope for your intimate relationship with God. Your soul seems too weary to fight through the darkness. Your may feel that your faith is weak, and God's presence distant.

Perhaps you have had moments where your spirit felt alive, where God seemed near, and you experienced vitality in your relationship with God. Now, however, you may feel disconnected from the source of life, struggling to find the motivation to pray, to seek God. Happiness seems to come and god and that eternal joy seems a distant possibility. David is expressing a deep spiritual weariness, where it feels like his strength to carry on following God's direction is slipping away.

When your spirit is troubled, you can call out to God for help. The very act of praying is a way of reaching out to God, showing that you still trust in Him to revive and strengthen you. Remember that God's grace is always available to uplift your spirit, even when it feels weak or overwhelmed. When it feels like your spirit faints, it is a reminder that you need God's intervention, His comfort, and His love to renew you, just as the body needs rest to regain its energy.

When you pray, "*My heart was troubled within me,*" you are again expressing this sense of inner turmoil about your spiritual condition in another way. The heart refers to your spiritual center, where the Holy Spirit works, and where a person encounters the divine.

St. Symeon the New Theologian (*Hymns of Divine Love*):

> "The heart is the place where we meet Christ. It is there that He makes His home."

Orthodoxy teaches that the heart must be purified and sanctified through prayer, repentance, and participation in the sacraments to be in right communion with God. The goal is to allow God's grace to transform the heart, leading to the theosis (deification) process, where a person becomes united with God's divine nature. Too often, you feel troubled, unsettled, and unable to find peace.

This feeling of your heart being "*troubled*" and your spirit being in "*anguish*" indicates that you have recognized your true spiritual condition. This can feel very distressing, causing a shock or an emotional reaction. David is conveying a sense of being struck with dismay or fear, feeling emotionally or spiritually undone by the spiritual condition he faces.

Yet, even in the midst of feeling "*troubled*," you can turn to God like David, expressing your spiritual struggles. This honest outpouring is part of the healing process. By bringing your troubled heart before God, you are inviting Him into your condition, trusting that He will provide comfort, healing, love, and guidance. Even when your heart is appalled, God's mercy can reach deep into your soul, bringing peace where there is fear and dismay. When you connect with Him, He can heal your condition and bring you great joy in the midst of your daily activities.

5. I remembered the days of old,
And I meditated on all Your works;
I meditated on the works of Your hands.

The "*days of old*," most likely refers to the times in the past when David experienced a closer, more intimate relationship with God—a time when he felt God's presence more strongly, when his faith was more vibrant, and when his life was marked by a greater sense of spiritual vitality and peace.

The "*days of old*" can also refer to the history of God's covenant with His people—the times of the patriarchs, the Exodus, and the many moments throughout Israel's history when God showed His faithfulness to His people. David may be recalling the mighty acts of God in these earlier times, particularly as seen in the stories of salvation history. These memories, both personal and communal, remind him of God's enduring faithfulness and encourage him to continue trusting in God's mercy.

When you think of the days of old, think of the time when you experienced God's presence and how you were filled with joy.. This is what comes with a pure heart, deep faith, and longing to live a life that is Christ-like.

"I meditated on all Your works," suggests turning your focus toward the many ways God has shown His faithfulness, power, and mercy throughout your life. In times of trial or spiritual exhaustion, this meditation becomes a source of strength. You want to fill your mind with God's goodness and reject ruminating about past troubles. Otherwise, you may feel overwhelmed by your past struggles. Here, you are asked to think about how God has always been present—guiding you, protecting you, and answering your prayers.

You can also reflect on the Scripture and how from Creation to this day, God has been guiding humanity toward union with Him. Think about the Exodus from Egypt; the Incarnation that led to the Crucifixion and then the Resurrection. This Biblical history is meant for this kind of reflection.

"I meditated on the works of Your hands" carries a more intimate and contemplative connotation, focusing specifically on the work of God's hands, which emphasizes His personal involvement in creation and the salvation of His people.

To meditate means to reflect deeply, to ponder, or to contemplate thoughtfully, often with a sense of awe and reverence. David is reflecting not only on the events or deeds of God but also on the craftsmanship and intentionality behind His actions. God's "hands" symbolize His active role in creation, in your life, and in salvation history. You are acknowledging that every aspect of His work is deliberate, perfect, and filled with divine wisdom.

When you meditate on all that God has done, open your heart to gratitude and hope. You see how God's hand has shaped your life, guiding you toward growth and healing, to become like Him. This encourages you to trust that the same God, who was present with you in the past, is with you now, ready to help you through whatever comes. This meditation is an invitation to align your heart with His divine will, allowing the memory of His past faithfulness to fuel your confidence in His ongoing care and love.

6. I spread out my hands to You;
My soul thirsts for You like a waterless land.

When you pray, *"I spread out my hands to You,"* you are expressing a deep, personal plea for God's help and presence. The act of stretching out your hands symbolizes a posture of vulnerability, surrender, and longing. It is a physical and spiritual gesture that acknowledges your dependence on God. In the same way that a child reaches out to a parent, or as you reach out to embrace a good friend, you are reaching out to God, asking for His embrace, His guidance, and His strength.

In moments of spiritual dryness, despair, or confusion, this act of stretching out your hands is a powerful reminder that God is always available to you, and that you can turn to Him at any time for strength and guidance. It is an expression of your relationship with God, rooted in trust and humility, recognizing that only God can provide what you truly need.

"My soul thirsts" speaks to the soul's intrinsic desire to be united with God, to experience His love, and to receive His salvation. This thirst is an acknowledgment that apart from God, your soul remains unsatisfied and empty. David's expression of thirst reflects spiritual dryness, often caused by the absence of God's presence, hardship, or feelings of abandonment. Yet, it is also a hopeful plea that God will quench this thirst, as He alone is the true source of living water.

In the New Testament, Jesus picks up this imagery when He says,

> "If anyone thirsts, let him come to Me and drink.
> He who believes in Me, as the Scripture has said,
> out of his heart will flow rivers of living water."
> (John 7:37–38)

Here, Jesus offers Himself as the living water that satisfies the soul's deepest thirst. Thus, when you say, "*My soul thirsts*," you are expressing a spiritual hunger for God, a deep craving for His presence, and a desire for His grace to transform and fill you.

Just as a "*waterless land*" suffers without rain, your soul may feel dry, weary, and empty without God's nourishing presence. This thirsting is not just a casual desire but an urgent need. Like someone in the desert, deprived of water, your thirst becomes intense, even life-preserving. Only God, in His infinite love and mercy, can quench the thirst of your soul.

God invites you to approach Him in this spiritual thirst, trusting that He will quench it with His living water—the Holy Spirit, His Word, and His grace. When you feel spiritually dry or empty, this prayer serves as a reminder to turn to God, to seek His presence, and to trust that He will satisfy your soul's deepest needs.

7. Hear me speedily, O Lord;
My spirit faints within me;
Turn not Your face from me,
Lest I become like those who go down into the pit.

"*My spirit faints within me*" indicates a spiritual weariness in the face of life's trials, struggles, or burdens. It indicates feeling as though you are spiritually dry and find it difficult to draw closer to God. You feel a need for God's intervention to restore you.

The weight of sin, suffering, or even the feeling of God's distance can contribute to this sense of spiritual exhaustion. When you feel abandoned by God or unsure of where to turn, and your soul longs for His comfort and strength, you are acknowledging that only God can provide what is necessary for your survival—spiritually, emotionally, or physically.

This cry for God to "*Hear me speedily,*" indicates you believe that God is always present, even when His response seems delayed. His timing is always perfect, but your longing for His quick action reveals your faith in His ability to provide for your needs. The urgency you express is not a lack of trust in God, but an honest admission of your frailty and your dependence on His mercy.

When you pray, "*Turn not Your face from me, lest I become like those who go down into the pit,*" you are expressing a fear of being abandoned by God. Asking God not to hide His face is a plea for His presence. In Scripture, God's "*face*" often symbolizes His favor, His attention, and His love. When God "turns His face" away, it signifies a sense of distance, separation, or absence.

Lord spoke to Moses, telling him how to bless the children of Israel:

> "The Lord bless you and keep you; the Lord make
> His face to shine upon you and be gracious to you;
> the Lord lift up His countenance upon you and give
> you peace." (Numbers 6:24–26)

Here, the "shining face" of God is a blessing, indicating His grace and favor toward His people. God's face is associated with His presence, which brings peace, security, and spiritual life.

The "*pit*" in the Old Testament is represented in terms like the abyss (Greek: abyssos) and Tartarus in the New Testament. These terms reflect places of spiritual ruin, judgment, and separation from God, much like the "*pit*" in the Old Testament imagery, which is associated with death, despair, and destruction.

The New Testament emphasizes that Christ's resurrection brings hope and deliverance from these places of spiritual darkness.

Fearing that you may be trodden into the "*pit*," indicates an awareness that you are vulnerable to the forces of sin, despair, and spiritual death. Your plea is a recognition that only God's nearness can prevent you from falling into that state of utter separation from Him.

8. Cause me to hear Your mercy in the morning,
For I hope in You;
Make me know, O Lord, the way wherein
I should walk,
For I lift up my soul to You.

Why would we say, "*Cause me hear Your mercy in the morning*"? The morning is renewal. The light of the sun overtakes the darkness of night waking us from sleep to a fresh new day. This is a parallel of Christ, who comes as light to lead you out of a worldly life, when He seemed distant and you were lost in darkness. Seeking God first thing in the morning as you awake is a way of expressing your desire to be spiritually renewed. It is a chance to start the day with a fresh encounter with God.

In the morning, everything is quiet—your external environment is calm. There is no din of traffic or voices in your home, and having just awakened from a night's sleep, your physical being is still. Your mind and heart are undisturbed. By turning to God first thing, you, like David, can more easily center your thoughts on God's will and invite divine clarity to help face the challenges ahead.

Just as your body needs nourishment in the morning, your soul needs spiritual nourishment.

When you begin the day in prayer, you prepare yourself to do God's will that day. It is an act of dependence—acknowledging that only God can equip you for what lies ahead. You place your trust in Him to guide and strengthen you as you face the day's trials. You are proclaiming your love for God, seeking His divine light to shine in you, just as the sun rises in the east to bring light to the whole world.

"Make me know, O Lord, the way wherein I should walk," expresses a deep longing for God's guidance and wisdom in your life. This plea is not just about seeking direction for a single decision but about asking God to shape your path, your choices, and your life in accordance with His will. It is an acknowledgment that, in your own strength and understanding, you may not always know the right way, and you need God's help to navigate the complexities of life.

Jesus says:

> "I am the way, and the truth, and the life. No one comes to the Father except through Me." (John 14:6)

The "way" you are asking God to teach you is not just a set of practical steps but a way of living that aligns with His divine will and reflects His holiness. You embrace the desire for theosis, an intimate union with God that prepares you for eternal life in His kingdom. It is the way of love, humility, patience, and grace—the way that leads to deeper communion with God.

You are inviting God into every aspect of your journey, seeking His direction in your relationships, work, spiritual life, and every choice you make. You are trusting that, through prayer, Scripture, the guidance of the Church, and the wisdom of the saints, God will reveal His way to you—whether through direct guidance, quiet conviction, or peaceful assurance.

Ultimately, this verse is about a deeper relationship with God. It is a request to walk closely with Him, to be attentive to His voice, and to trust in His leading as He teaches you the way, one step at a time.

9. Deliver me from my enemies, O Lord, For to You I flee for refuge.

Spiritually, your enemies are not the people, forces, and societal norms that oppose your desires, but temptations, inner turmoil, or even overwhelming circumstances that threaten your peace and well-being, and cloud your soul.

"Deliver me from my enemies. O Lord" is a cry for divine help as you face the challenges of your worldly life. It reflects your desire to overcome the forces that pull you away from God's will, hindering your spiritual growth.

By seeking *"refuge"* in God, you are recognizing that you cannot face these challenges on your own. The word *"refuge"* signifies a place of safety, a sanctuary where you can find shelter. Spiritually, it is a condition where you experience God's protection and peace in the midst of distress.

Jesus invites you to come to Him for refuge and rest during times of trouble. He offers not only physical protection but spiritual peace, encouraging you to find refuge in Him, where our souls can be at rest. He says,

> "Come to Me, all you who labor and are heavy laden, and I will give you rest. Take My yoke upon you, and learn from Me, for I am gentle and lowly in heart, and you will find rest for your souls. For My yoke is easy, and My burden is light." (Matthew 11:28–30)

In the Old Testament, God was a refuge for Israel during times of distress. The Bible repeatedly assures you that God is a stronghold, rock, and fortress (Psalm 18:2), offering protection from both physical and spiritual enemies. By praying this, you are reaffirming your trust in God's ability to protect you and deliver you from harm.

The apostle Paul writes,

> "But the Lord is faithful. He will establish you and guard you against the evil one." (2 Thessalonians 3:3)

In this verse, Paul reassures you that God is faithful to protect you, guarding you against the influence and attacks of the enemy.

James says,

> "Submit yourselves therefore to God. Resist the devil, and he will flee from you." (James 4:7)

He is saying that through submission to God and resistance of the devil, God delivers you from spiritual oppression and provides the strength to overcome temptations.

Jesus is our protector and offers you safety from sin, temptation, and external threats. The New Testament reassures you that no matter the trials you face, God is always your refuge. It is in Christ that you have access to divine protection and salvation. By seeking Him in faith, you trust that He will deliver you from evil, guide you through difficulties, and grant you peace that surpasses all understanding.

By praying, "*Deliver me from my enemies O Lord, for to You I flee for refuge,*" you are expressing your complete dependence on God as your protector and Savior, acknowledging that only in Him can you find true safety, peace, and deliverance.

10. Teach me to do Your will, for You are my God; Your good Spirit shall guide me in the land of uprightness.

11. For Your name's sake, O Lord, give me life; In Your righteousness, You shall bring my soul out of affliction.

12. In Your mercy, You shall destroy my enemies; You shall utterly destroy all who afflict my soul, For I am Your servant.

Summary

When you recite this psalm prayerfully, you are inviting God into your life, acknowledging both His greatness and His nearness. This is not just about asking for help—it's about seeking a deeper relationship with God, trusting in His unchanging faithfulness and perfect justice. You recognize your need for His grace and guidance, knowing that only through Him can you find peace, strength, and direction.

By humbling yourself before God and asking for His mercy and forgiveness, you acknowledge that salvation comes only through His grace, not your own merit, and trust that He will lead you toward repentance and healing.

By acknowledging your vulnerability and turning to God for deliverance, you demonstrate trust that, just as He has delivered His people in the past, He will intervene in your life, lift you up from despair, and restore your soul.

Praying in the quiet of the morning, you begin each day centered on God's presence, seeking His guidance and strength. This morning prayer is an opportunity to realign your heart with His will and invite His transforming grace into your life.

By inviting God to guide every aspect of your life, asking Him to lead you in righteousness, humility, and love, you open your heart to God's transformative power, trusting that He will guide you through all of life's challenges and lead you to a deeper, more faithful relationship with Him.